Vintage Modern KNITS

Contemporary designs using classic techniques

COURTNEY KELLEY & KATE GAGNON OSBORN

INTERWEAVE.
interweave.com

EDITOR Ann Budd
TECHNICAL EDITOR Karen Frisa
ART DIRECTOR Liz Quan
COVER AND INTERIOR DESIGN Karla Baker
MODEL PHOTOGRAPHER Joe Hancock
LANDSCAPE PHOTOGRAPHER Lynn Osborn
PHOTO STYLIST Carol Beaver
HAIR AND MAKEUP Kathy MacKay
PRODUCTION Katherine Jackson

Interweave Press LLC
201 East Fourth Street
Loveland, CO 80537-5655 USA
Interweave.com

Printed in China by Asia Pacific Offset Ltd.

Library of Congress Cataloging-in-Publication Data

Kelley, Courtney.
 Vintage modern knits : contemporary designs
using classic techniques / Courtney Kelley and Kate
Gagnon Osborn.
   p. cm.
 Includes index.
ISBN 978-1-59668-240-5 (pbk.)
ISBN 978-1-59668-492-8 (eBook)
1. Knitting--Patterns. 2. Women's clothing. I.
Osborn, Kate Gagnon. II. Title.
 TT825.K445 2010
 746.43'2--dc22

                  2010025828

10 9 8 7 6 5 4 3 2 1

WITHDRAWN

This book is dedicated with much love to Julia Ann, Lucy, Yvette, and Verna, our very patient grandmothers, who taught us a love of needle arts at a young age.

ACKNOWLEDGMENTS

We would like to extend our deepest thanks to all of the wonderful people at Interweave for making our vision a reality. We couldn't have done it without Tricia Waddell, who put the bee in our bonnets to write a book, and Ann Budd, our patient and phenomenal editor, who guided us through every step of the process.

All of our love and thanks go to our dear and supportive families who made our dinners, went on countless dog walks, clocked many hours of childcare, and put up with watching endless movies during the long winter as we frantically knit and wrote the patterns for this book at every possible spare moment.

A very special thanks goes to Iain and Daphne, for creating an amazing yarn company and putting the trust of its continuation in our hands. We will always be in awe of your creativity, forward thinking, artistic vision, and organization and forever grateful for the opportunity to work with Fibre Company yarns every day.

And to those with the most thankless job of all, the test and sample knitters: Jennifer May, Abby Wheeler, Lisa R. Myers, Daphane Marinpoulos, and Jenna Wilbur. Your patience and hard work—usually demanded at the last minute and with little reward—are what made much of this book possible.

CONTENTS

INTRODUCTION

The advent of electronic technology and the speed of the Internet have educated and joined the regions of our world together in ways heretofore unheard of. This hyperconnectivity has made it possible for individuals to access information that would have previously required years of research and apprenticeship. With this in mind, we wanted to provide a book that enabled the knitter to take some time to delve into the craftsmanship behind the vast history of our shared pastime. While this book, the projects, our inspiration, and our research was aided by the ability to access hard-to-find information online, it also pays direct homage to a time when life moved a little slower, and things were made to last.

High-quality items produced in small batches and meant to last well beyond a season or fashion trend (through generations, even) and attention to detail seemingly no longer hold value in our fast-paced consumer-driven society that values disposable goods and trendy fashion. However, the handmade has prevailed with its ability to tap into world traditions and continues to engage us in a celebration of knitting archives. The charm and beauty of the handmade sweater has stood the test of time, moving from necessity to practicality to simple hobby. While machines and manufacturing have brought all the comforts of our modern world, knitters find satisfaction in delving into the past and discovering that what was once a necessary means to keep the masses warm has become something that inspires, motivates, and moves us to be better in all that we do.

At the core, our individual aesthetics differ. Kate tends to hold firmly—if not with a bit of irony—to her New England roots, where practicality is paramount and multiple layers are a must (especially if there is a stripe or two in there). Courtney, instead, is inspired by the romance of history's necessity for handcrafts—always scouring flea markets for the handmade, much worn, and often repaired item, regardless of its usefulness. However, we always agree when we find ourselves at the intersection between tradition and modern styling. Our appreciation for vintage cuts, shapes, and techniques in knitting—fine-gauge Fair Isle patterning, intricate lace shawls, and allover cabling—transcends our disparate personal aesthetics. When daydreaming about knitwear designs and bouncing ideas off one another, we pull inspiration from similar sources and eventually find a balance between vintage and contemporary, practicality and sentiment. Whether choosing a slightly larger yarn gauge, including waist shaping, adding a twist to a style, or modifying construction, we love to update vintage-inspired knitwear to create a look of timelessness.

This book is the culmination of our shared love of tradition and the desire to make it contemporary. Each original project has its roots in a particular style or technique that has been updated for a modern application and aesthetic. As a whole, you'll find a collection that embodies our personal tastes, styles, and appreciation for the handmade. We hope that these projects inspire you to try something different, learn a new technique, and create timeless pieces of your own.

RUSTIC WEEKEND

AS SUMMER FADES, the breeze turns from soft and warm to cool and sharp with the weight of departure. Autumn evokes memory—the lingering scents of warmth. It weaves images of the changing landscape; the tapestry of leaves along the mountainside changes from green to gold, crimson, and finally brown.

Imagine a patchwork of valley farms busy with the last days of summer harvest; walk through the woods as the leaves fall and acorns crunch underfoot. The shortening days, crisp dry leaves, and the damp earth speak to the need for soft sweaters, unwrapped from tissue-paper cocoons after their summer hibernation.

The transition from warm days to chilly nights requires a versatile wardrobe with many layers. The projects in this collection focus on ways to keep warm while celebrating the history of knitting as the perfect marriage of function and form: a Faroese shawl to wrap around your shoulders while sitting by the fire on a fall's evening; warm Fair Isle kneesocks paired with summer's favorite jean skirt; a short-sleeved sweater to wear over a lightweight long-sleeved tee; and more. All of the garments and accessories in this section pay tribute to the useful industry of handknitting in its purest form.

Brigid JACKET

DESIGNED BY COURTNEY KELLEY

Inspired by the grassy plains, curving rivers, and rugged mountains of the Irish landscape, Aran sweaters have a long history. Many believe they harken from the days of family clans and sailors washed ashore—you can purchase a "historical" Aran sweater named for a particular family or clan. However, all of these designs were most likely created by a single knitter for the tourist trade. The Brigid Jacket pays homage to those traditional Aran cardigans as well as the duffle coats of the 1970s and 1980s (themselves a new interpretation of their time). This cropped version features an updated color, large cables up the fronts, a wide-rib buttonband, and three bold buttons, complementing the organic and rustic look.

MATERIALS

yarn
Worsted weight (#4 Medium).

shown here: The Fibre Company Terra (40% baby alpaca, 40% merino wool, 20% silk; 98 yd [91 m]/50 g): olive leaf, 8 (9, 10, 12, 13) skeins.

needles
Size U.S. 8 (5 mm).

Adjust needle size if necessary to obtain the correct gauge.

notions
Cable needle (cn); markers (m); stitch holder; tapestry needle; three 1½" (3.8 cm) buttons.

gauge
16 stitches and 24 rows = 4" (10 cm) in stockinette stitch.

20-stitch cable panel = 3" (7.5 cm).

finished size
About 36 (40, 44, 48, 52)" (91.5 [101.5, 112, 122, 132] cm) bust circumference. Jacket shown measures 40" (101.5 cm).

Note

> When shaping the front neck, if there are not enough stitches to work a cable cross, work these stitches in reverse stockinette stitch.

Sloped Bind-Off

To work a sloped bind-off when shaping the shoulder or neck (or any other shaping for that matter!), slip the first stitch of the bind-off as follows: Slip 1 stitch, work 1 stitch, pass the slipped stitch over the worked stitch—1 stitch has been bound off. The slipped stitch is one row shorter than if it had been worked, which causes the fabric to angle slightly and creates a sleeker bind-off edge. For the Brigid Jacket in particular, the single decreases in the neck shaping are worked by binding off 1 stitch instead of working a k2tog or ssk. Working single-stitch bind-offs while slipping the first bound-off stitch creates a smoother transition between rows, which makes it easier to pick up stitches for the collar.

Back

CO 72 (80, 88, 96, 104) sts. Work in k1, p1 rib for 1 (WS) row.

NEXT ROW: (RS) *K4, p4; rep from *.

Cont in k4, p4 rib as established until piece measures 2" (5 cm) from CO, ending with a WS row. Change to St st and work even until piece measures 9¼ (11¼, 10¾, 13½, 12¾)" (23.5 [28.5, 27.5, 34.5, 32.5] cm) from CO, ending with a WS row.

Shape Armholes

BO 4 (4, 4, 6, 6) sts at beg of next 2 rows—64 (72, 80, 84, 92) sts rem.

DEC ROW: (RS) K1, ssk, knit to last 3 sts, k2tog, k1—2 sts dec'd.

Purl 1 (WS) row. Dec 1 st each end of needle in this manner every RS row 2 more times, then every 4th row 1 (2, 2, 2, 3) more time(s)—56 (62, 70, 74, 80) sts rem. Work even until armholes measure 6 (6½, 7, 7, 7½)" (15 [16.5, 18, 18, 19] cm), ending with a WS row.

Shape Shoulders and Neck

With RS facing, k17 (20, 22, 24, 26) for right shoulder, place next 22 (22, 26, 26, 28) sts on holder to work later for back neck, leave rem 17 (20, 22, 24, 26) sts on needle to work later for left shoulder.

Right Shoulder and Neck

ROW 1: (WS) Sl 1, purl to end.

ROW 2: K14 (17, 19, 21, 23), k2tog, k1—16 (19, 21, 23, 25) sts rem.

ROWS 3 AND 5: Sl 1, purl to end.

ROW 4: BO 6 (6, 6, 7, 9) sts, knit to last 3 sts, k2tog, k1—9 (12, 14, 15, 15) sts rem.

ROW 6: BO 4 (6, 6, 7, 7) sts, knit to last 3 sts, k2tog, k1—4 (5, 7, 7, 7) sts rem.

ROW 7: Sl 1, purl to end.

BO all sts.

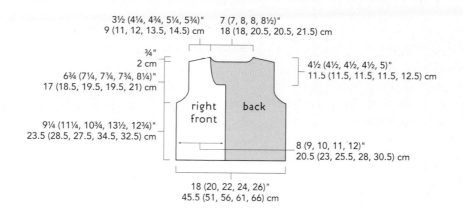

3½ (4¼, 4¾, 5¼, 5¾)"
9 (11, 12, 13.5, 14.5) cm

7 (7, 8, 8, 8½)"
18 (18, 20.5, 20.5, 21.5) cm

¾"
2 cm

4½ (4½, 4½, 4½, 5)"
11.5 (11.5, 11.5, 11.5, 12.5) cm

6¾ (7¼, 7¾, 7¾, 8¼)"
17 (18.5, 19.5, 19.5, 21) cm

right front   back

9¼ (11¼, 10¾, 13½, 12¾)"
23.5 (28.5, 27.5, 34.5, 32.5) cm

8 (9, 10, 11, 12)"
20.5 (23, 25.5, 28, 30.5) cm

18 (20, 22, 24, 26)"
45.5 (51, 56, 61, 66) cm

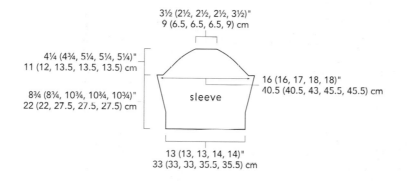

3½ (2½, 2½, 2½, 3½)"
9 (6.5, 6.5, 6.5, 9) cm

4¼ (4¾, 5¼, 5¼, 5¼)"
11 (12, 13.5, 13.5, 13.5) cm

16 (16, 17, 18, 18)"
40.5 (40.5, 43, 45.5, 45.5) cm

8¾ (8¾, 10¾, 10¾, 10¾)"
22 (22, 27.5, 27.5, 27.5) cm

sleeve

13 (13, 13, 14, 14)"
33 (33, 33, 35.5, 35.5) cm

Cable

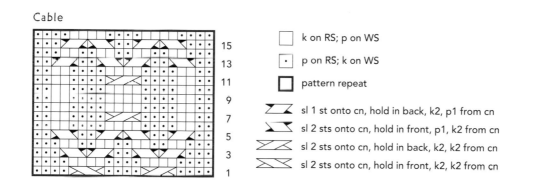

15
13
11
9
7
5
3
1

☐ k on RS; p on WS

• p on RS; k on WS

☐ pattern repeat

sl 1 st onto cn, hold in back, k2, p1 from cn

sl 2 sts onto cn, hold in front, p1, k2 from cn

sl 2 sts onto cn, hold in back, k2, k2 from cn

sl 2 sts onto cn, hold in front, k2, k2 from cn

Left Shoulder and Neck

Rejoin yarn to left shoulder sts at armhole edge.

ROW 1: (WS) P17 (20, 22, 24, 26).

ROWS 2, 4, AND 6: Sl 1, knit to end.

ROW 3: P14 (17, 19, 21, 23), ssp (see Glossary), p1—16 (19, 21, 23, 25) sts rem.

ROW 5: BO 6 (6, 6, 7, 9) sts, purl to last 3 sts, ssp, p1—9 (12, 14, 15, 15) sts rem.

ROW 7: BO 4 (6, 6, 7, 7) sts, purl to last 3 sts, ssp, p1—4 (5, 7, 7, 7) sts rem.

ROW 8: Sl 1, knit to end.

BO all sts.

Right Front

CO 40 (44, 48, 52, 56) sts.

ROW 1: (WS) *P1, k1; rep from *.

ROW 2: (RS) *K4, p4; rep from * to last 0 (4, 0, 4, 0) sts, k0 (4, 0, 4, 0).

ROW 3: P0 (4, 0, 4, 0), *k4, p4; rep from *.

Rep Rows 2 and 3 until piece measures 2" (5 cm) from CO, ending with a WS row.

SET-UP ROW: (RS) K4 (4, 4, 4, 8), work Row 1 of Cable chart over next 20 sts, k16 (20, 24, 28, 28).

Cont as established, working Cable chart over 20 sts and rem sts in St st, until chart Rows 1–16 have been worked 2 (3, 3, 4, 4) times total, then work Row(s) 1–11 (1–7, 1–5, 1–5, 1 only) once more—piece measures about 9¼ (11¼, 10¾, 13½, 12¾)" (23.5 [28.5, 27.5, 34.5, 32.5] cm) from CO.

Shape Armhole

With WS facing, BO 4 (4, 4, 6, 6) sts, work to end—36 (40, 44, 46, 50) sts rem. Work 1 RS row even.

DEC ROW: (WS) P1, p2tog, work in patt to end of row—1 st dec'd.

Rep the last 2 rows 2 more times—33 (37, 41, 43, 47) sts rem. Rep dec row every 4th row 1 (2, 2, 2, 3) time(s)—32 (35, 39, 41, 44) sts rem. Work even through Row 12 (12, 12, 12, 10) of chart.

Shape Neck

Size 52" (132 cm) only

(Row 11 of chart) BO 4 sts, work to end of row—40 sts rem. Work Row 12 of chart.

All Sizes

Keeping in patt (see Notes), at neck edge (beg of RS rows), BO 4 sts once, then BO 2 sts 2 times—24 (27, 31, 33, 32) sts rem. BO 1 st at neck edge once—23 (26, 30, 32, 31) sts rem. Work 3 rows even in patt, ending with chart Row 6. BO 1 st at neck edge on next row, then every 4th row 3 more times—19 (22, 26, 28, 27) sts rem.

Shape Shoulder

ROW 1: (WS) BO 6 (6, 6, 7, 9) sts, work to end—13 (16, 20, 21, 18) sts rem.

ROWS 2 AND 4: Sl 1, work to end of row.

ROW 3: BO 6 (8, 8, 9, 9) sts, work to end—7 (8, 12, 12, 9) sts rem.

With WS facing, BO rem sts.

Left Front

CO 40 (44, 48, 52, 56) sts.

ROW 1: (WS) *K1, p1; rep from *.

ROW 2: (RS) K0 (4, 0, 4, 0), *p4, k4; rep from *.

ROW 3: *P4, k4; rep from * to last 0 (4, 0, 4, 0) sts, p0 (4, 0, 4, 0).

Rep Rows 2 and 3 until piece measures 2" (5 cm) from CO, ending with a WS row.

SET-UP ROW: (RS) K16 (20, 24, 28, 28), work Row 1 of Cable chart over next 20 sts, k4 (4, 4, 4, 8).

Cont as established, working Cable chart over 20 sts and rem sts in St st, until chart Rows 1–16 have been worked 2 (3, 3, 4, 3) times total, then work Rows 1–10 (1–6, 1–4, 1–4, 1–16) once more.

Shape Armhole

With RS facing, BO 4 (4, 4, 6, 6) sts, work to end—36 (40, 44, 46, 50) sts rem. Work 1 WS row even.

DEC ROW: (RS) K1, ssk, work in patt to end of row—1 st dec'd.

Rep the last 2 rows 2 more times—33 (37, 41, 43, 47) sts rem. Rep dec row every 4th row 1 (2, 2, 2, 3) time(s)—32 (35, 39, 41, 44) sts rem. Work even through Row 13 (13, 13, 13, 11) of chart.

Shape Neck

Size 52" (132 cm) only
(Row 12 of chart) BO 4 sts, work to end of row—40 sts rem. Work Row 13 of chart.

All Sizes
Keeping in patt (see Notes), at neck edge (beg of WS rows), BO 4 sts once, then BO 2 sts 2 times—24 (27, 31, 33, 32) sts rem. BO 1 st at neck edge once—23 (26, 30, 32, 31) sts rem. Work 3 rows even in patt, ending with chart Row 7. BO 1 st at neck edge on next row, then every 4th row 3 more times—19 (22, 26, 28, 27) sts rem.

Shape Shoulder

ROW 1: (RS) BO 6 (6, 6, 7, 9) sts, work to end of row—13 (16, 20, 21, 18) sts rem.

ROWS 2 AND 4: (WS) Sl 1, work to end of row.

ROW 3: BO 6 (8, 8, 9, 9) sts, work to end of row—7 (8, 12, 12, 9) sts rem.

With RS facing, BO rem sts.

Sleeves

CO 52 (52, 52, 56, 56) sts. Work in k2, p2 rib until piece measures 2" (5 cm) from CO, ending with a WS row. Change to St st and work 4 rows even.

INC ROW: (RS) K1f&b (see Glossary), knit to last 2 sts, k1f&b, k1—2 sts inc'd.

Work 5 rows even. Rep the last 6 rows 5 (5, 7, 7, 7) more times—64 (64, 68, 72, 72) sts; piece measures about 8¾ (8¾, 10¾, 10¾, 10¾)" (22 [22, 27.5, 27.5, 27.5] cm) from CO.

Shape Cap

BO 4 (4, 4, 6, 6) sts at beg of next 2 rows—56 (56, 60, 60, 60) sts rem.

DEC ROW: (RS) K1, ssk, knit to last 3 sts, k2tog, k1—2 sts dec'd.

Purl 1 WS row. Dec 1 st each end of needle in this manner every RS row 5 (7, 7, 7, 9) more times, then dec every row 6 (6, 8, 8, 4) times, working WS dec rows as p1, p2tog, purl to last 3 sts, ssp, p1—32 (28, 28, 28, 32) sts rem after all dec's have been worked.

NEXT ROW: (WS) BO 2 sts (see box on page 12), purl to last 3 sts, ssp, p1—3 sts dec'd.

NEXT ROW: BO 2 sts, knit to last 3 sts, k2tog, k1—3 sts dec'd.

Rep the last 2 rows 2 more times—14 (10, 10, 10, 14) sts rem.

BO all sts.

Finishing

Block pieces to measurements. With yarn threaded on a tapestry needle, sew shoulder seams, easing front shoulders as necessary. Sew sleeve caps into armholes. Sew sleeve and side seams.

Front Bands

With RS facing and beg at lower edge, pick up and knit 60 (68, 68, 76, 76) sts evenly spaced along right front edge.

SET-UP ROW: (WS) P4, *k4, p4; rep from *.

Work in k4, p4 rib for 4 more rows.

BUTTONHOLE ROW 1: (RS) Work 28 (36, 36, 44, 44) sts in rib as established, p1, BO 2 sts, p1, k4, p4, k4, p1, BO 2 sts, p1, k4, p4, k4.

BUTTONHOLE ROW 2: (WS) Working in rib as established, use the backward-loop method (see Glossary) to CO 2 sts over each gap formed on previous row.

Cont in rib as established for 5 more rows. BO all sts in patt.

Rep for left front edge, omitting buttonholes.

Collar

With RS facing and beg at edge of right front band, pick up and knit 23 (23, 25, 25, 28) sts along neck edge to shoulder, k22 (22, 26, 26, 28) held back neck sts, pick up and knit 23 (23, 25, 25, 28) sts along neck edge to end of left front band—68 (68, 76, 76, 84) sts total.

NEXT ROW: (WS) P4, *k4, p4; rep from *.

Cont in k4, p4 rib as established for 2 more rows.

BUTTONHOLE ROW 1: (RS) K4, p1, BO 2 sts, p1, work in rib as established to end of row.

BUTTONHOLE ROW 2: (WS) Working in rib as established, use the backward-loop method to CO 2 sts over gap formed on previous row.

Cont in rib as established for 3 more rows. BO all sts in patt.

Weave in loose ends.

Madeleine SHAWL

DESIGNED BY COURTNEY KELLEY

This pretty picot-edged shawl is a great traveling or weekend project. It is knitted point to point in a garter-based bias-stitch pattern that is worked simultaneously with the picot edge. The construction is simple enough for beginners and interesting enough to keep advanced knitters engrossed. The bias pattern creates a Faroese-style wing to shape the points, which allows the shawl to drape comfortably around the shoulders. Knitted in a worsted-weight luxury yarn, this shawl mixes the practical warmth of a thick homespun peddler's shawl with the softness of a fine Regency-era cashmere shawl. Endlessly customizable and requiring fewer than 300 yards (275 meters) of yarn, this shawl is ideal for quick gifts and using up that odd skein or two of yarn.

MATERIALS

yarn
Worsted weight (#4 Medium).

shown here: The Fibre Company Road to China (65% baby alpaca, 15% silk, 10% camel, 10% cashmere; 69 yd [63 m]/50 g): jade, 4 skeins.

needles
Size U.S. 10 (6 mm).

Adjust needle size if necessary to obtain the correct gauge.

notions
Tapestry needle.

gauge
About 11 stitches and 18 rows = 4" (10 cm) in bias-stitch pattern.

finished size
About 54" (137 cm) wide and 24" (61 cm) long at point.

Make Picot (MP)

Using the cable method (see Glossary), CO 3 sts. Working the first st through the back loop, BO 3 sts.

Designing Bias-Stitch Patterns

In woven fabrics, the lengthwise grain is the direction of the warp threads that run vertically along the fabric, and the widthwise grain is the direction of the weft threads that run horizontally across the fabric. The bias is measured at 45 degrees to the vertical and horizontal, or diagonally across the fabric. Garments constructed on the bias will have more stretch and hang with more drape than garments constructed on the lengthwise or widthwise grain. Knitted fabrics can also be constructed on the bias to maximize drape. Achieved through the creative use of increases on one side of the work paired with decreases on the other side, a rectangular fabric can be created in which the stitches slant to the left or right. The increases add fabric to one edge while the decreases remove fabric from the other. This produces a fabric that hangs beautifully and is particularly effective for shawls and wraps.

The direction of bias depends on the placement of the increases and decreases. If the increases are worked at the beginning of right-side rows and the decreases are worked at the end these rows, the fabric will slant toward the left. If the increases are worked at the end of right-side rows and the decreases are worked at the beginning of these rows, the fabric will slant toward the right.

The stitch pattern for the first half of this shawl is a simple repetition of ssk decreases followed by yarnover increases.

ROW 1: (RS) K1, *ssk, yo; rep from * to last 2 sts, k2.

ROW 2: (WS) Knit.

As these two rows are repeated, the yarnover increases and ssk decreases align vertically to form pillars. Because the decreases are worked before the increases, the fabric slants to the left.

For the second half of the shawl, the yarnover increases are followed by ssk decreases.

ROW 1: (RS) K2, *yo, ssk; rep from * to last st, k1.

ROW 2: (WS) Knit.

As these two rows are repeated, the fabric slants to the right because the increases are worked before the decreases.

A "V" forms where the stitch pattern changes direction, which is perfectly formed to cradle the nape of your neck.

Shawl

CO 2 sts.

SET-UP ROW 1: K1f&b (see Glossary), k1—3 sts.

SET-UP ROW 2: [K1f&b] 2 times, k1—5 sts.

Cont to inc in patt as foll:

ROW 1: Sl 1, *ssk, yo; rep from * to last 2 sts, k2.

ROW 2: MP (see Stitch Guide), k1f&b, knit to end—1 st inc'd.

ROW 3: Sl 1, *ssk, yo; rep from * to last 3 sts, k3.

ROW 4: K1f&b, knit to end—1 st inc'd.

Rep these 4 rows 29 more times, ending with Row 4—65 sts, 30 picots; piece measures about 27" (68.5 cm) from CO. Dec in patt as foll:

ROW 1: Sl 1, k1, *yo, ssk; rep from * to last 3 sts, k3.

ROW 2: MP, ssk, knit to end—1 st dec'd.

ROW 3: Sl 1, k1, *yo, ssk; rep from * to last 2 sts, k2.

ROW 4: Ssk, knit to end—1 st dec'd.

Rep these 4 rows 29 more times, ending with Row 4—5 sts rem.

NEXT ROW: Sl 1, k1, yo, ssk, k1.

NEXT ROW: Ssk, k3—4 sts rem.

NEXT ROW: Ssk, k2tog—2 sts rem.

BO rem 2 sts.

Finishing

Weave in loose ends. Steam-block to measurements.

Bramble BERET

DESIGNED BY COURTNEY KELLEY

This beret uses two traditional Aran patterns that are modified to be worked in the round. The blackberry stitch (also known as trinity stitch), a traditional filler stitch used at the seams or between larger motifs in Aran designs, is generally worked by increasing in each stitch on right-side rows, then decreasing on wrong-side rows. For this beret, however, the increases and decreases are worked on the same round, much the same as working bobbles. In addition, a double moss-stitch-filled cable pattern travels seamlessly over the beginning of the round to keep the pattern elements fluid. The crossing cables move in a diamond pattern, transecting the beginning of the round at their widest, then decreasing back down.

finished size
About 18¾" (47.5 cm) in circumference at brim, 28" (71 cm) in circumference at widest point, and 8" (20.5 cm) tall, after blocking.

MATERIALS

yarn
Worsted weight (#4 Medium).

shown here: The Fibre Company Canopy Worsted (50% baby alpaca, 30% merino, 20% bamboo, 100 yd [91 m]/50 g): laguna, 2 skeins.

needles
Ribbing: Size U.S. 5 (3.75 mm): 16" (40 cm) circular (cir).

Body: Size U.S. 7 (4.5 mm): 16" (40 cm) cir and set of 4 double-pointed (dpn).

Adjust needle size if necessary to obtain the correct gauge.

notions
Marker (m); two cable needles (cn); tapestry needle.

gauge
18 stitches and 28 rounds = 4" (10 cm) in pattern stitch on larger needles, worked in rounds.

Notes

> The marker is moved to accompany the beginning of the round beside the diamond cable. The marker should always fall before the k2 of the first diamond cable motif.

> Due to the traveling cable, the beginning of the round shifts 1 stitch to the right at the end of every even-numbered round for the first 12 rounds; the beginning of the round then shifts 1 stitch to the left at the beginning of every odd-numbered round for the next 13 rounds, then to the right again as the top is decreased.

> For even-numbered Rounds 2–12, work in pattern to 1 stitch before the end of the round. Work the first cable of the next round as: Sl last st of rnd onto cn and hold in back, sl m to right-hand needle, k2, p1 from cn. For odd-numbered Rounds 15–25, work the first cable as: Remove m at beg of rnd, sl 2 sts onto cn and hold in front, p1, replace m, k2 from cn.

> When working the chart, note that the beginning of the round is at the marker line, not at the right edge of the chart.

Hat

With smaller cir needle, CO 84 sts. Place marker (pm) and join for working in rnds, being careful not to twist sts.

NEXT RND: *[K2, p1] 2 times, [k1, p1] 3 times; rep from *.

Cont in rib as established until piece measures 1¾" (4.5 cm) from CO. Change to larger cir needle.

INC RND: *K2, p1, k2, p1, [M1 (see page 78), k1, M1, p1] 3 times; rep from *—126 sts.

Work Rnds 1–28 of Hat chart (see Notes)—piece measures about 5¾" (14.5 cm) from CO.

Shape Top

Work Rnds 1–16 of Crown chart, changing to dpn when there are too few sts to fit comfortably on cir needle—14 sts rem.

Finishing

Cut yarn, leaving a 10" (25.5 cm) tail. Thread tail on a tapestry needle, draw through rem sts, pull tight to close hole, and fasten off on WS.

Weave in loose ends. Block lightly.

Shifting the Beginning of the Round

When some patterns—cables in particular—are worked in the round, the beginning of the round has to shift from round to round to maintain the integrity of the cable crossings. In other words, the cables twist around one another throughout the entire round, regardless of where the round begins. I like to think of a cabled hat as a large circular Celtic knot, with no beginning or end—it twines around and around indefinitely. You do need to mark the beginning of the round to facilitate the written instructions and replication of the knitted item, but the beginning of the round, and the marker, will shift as the piece is worked.

Two patterns interact in this hat—a blackberry stitch and a cable that undulates open and closed around a moss-stitch center. At its narrowest point, the cable is 5 stitches wide and is worked once as a 2/1/2 LC. On the next round, the 5 stitches of the cable divide, and 2 are worked into a 2/1RPC and another 2 are worked into a 2/1LPC. Because the beginning of the round occurs at the beginning of those 5 cable stitches, the beginning shifts to the right with them. To track the beginning of the round, keep the marker in front of the 2/1RPC. Then, when the cable reaches its widest point and begins to narrow again (when the 2/1RPC evolves into a 2/1LPC), move the marker back to the left with these stitches.

Hat

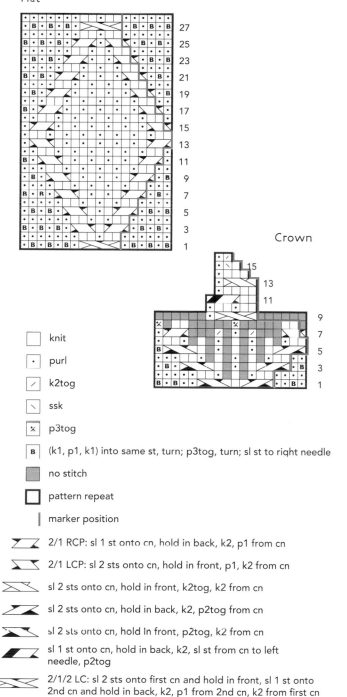

27
25
23
21
19
17
15
13
11
9
7
5
3
1

Crown

15
13
11
9
7
5
3
1

	knit
·	purl
⟋	k2tog
⟍	ssk
⅄	p3tog
B	(k1, p1, k1) into same st, turn; p3tog, turn; sl st to right needle
▦	no stitch
☐	pattern repeat
ǀ	marker position

2/1 RCP: sl 1 st onto cn, hold in back, k2, p1 from cn

2/1 LCP: sl 2 sts onto cn, hold in front, p1, k2 from cn

sl 2 sts onto cn, hold in front, k2tog, k2 from cn

sl 2 sts onto cn, hold in back, k2, p2tog from cn

sl 2 sts onto cn, hold in front, p2tog, k2 from cn

sl 1 st onto cn, hold in back, k2, sl st from cn to left
needle, p2tog

2/1/2 LC: sl 2 sts onto first cn and hold in front, sl 1 st onto
2nd cn and hold in back, k2, p1 from 2nd cn, k2 from first cn

Maple Bay CARDIGAN

DESIGNED BY COURTNEY KELLEY

Although only those sweaters made by the Coast Salish peoples of Canada's western coast can bear the official Cowichan moniker, this sweater takes inspiration from the traditional sweaters of that rugged region. The word Cowichan is derived from the Coast Salish Hul'qumi'num' word *Khowutzun* or *Quw'utsun'* (spellings vary), which means "land warmed by the sun." The traditional sweaters made by these tribes incorporate bold geometrics and natural imagery worked in bulky natural-colored wool in the intarsia method of color blocks. More fitted than the traditional bulky overcoat style, this version is knitted in a varied color palette in a blend of natural fibers that is soft and warm close to the skin.

MATERIALS

yarn
Worsted weight (#4 Medium).

shown here: The Fibre Company Organik (70% merino wool, 15% baby alpaca, 15% silk; 98 yd [90 m]/50 g): river delta (tan; MC), 9 (11, 12, 14) skeins; loam (dark brown; CC1), 3 skeins; highlands (blue-green; CC2), 2 skeins; arctic tundra (white; CC3), 2 (2, 2, 3) skeins.

needles
body: size U.S. 7 (4.5 mm).

cuffs and collar: size U.S. 6 (4 mm): straight and 32" (80 cm) cir.

Adjust needle size if necessary to obtain the correct gauge.

notions
Markers (m); stitch holders or waste yarn; four 2" (5 cm) toggle buttons; tapestry needle.

gauge
18 stitches and 27 rows = 4" (10 cm) in stockinette stitch on larger needles.

finished size
About 36 (38½, 43, 47)" (91.5 [98, 109, 119.5] cm) bust circumference.
Sweater shown measures 36" (91.5 cm).

Note

> The Triangles chart is worked using the stranded knitting method, using three colors on two of the rows. The Small Leaf, Large Leaf, and Beaver charts are worked using the intarsia method.

Intarsia

Intarsia is knitting with two or more colors to create a pattern motif. Unlike stranded knitting, no "floats" of nonworking yarn are carried across the back of the work in intarsia. Similar to tapestry weaving, intarsia is worked in blocks, or sections, of color across each row. The nonworking yarn hangs at the back until it is needed again on the next row. Some people find it easiest to work with a bobbin of yarn for each color block. I prefer to cut lengths 2 to 5 yards (1.8 to 4.5 meters) long for each block. The advantage is that the lengths can be easier to untangle than bobbins; the disadvantage is that there are more ends to weave in later. Whichever method you use, be sure to twist the working and nonworking yarns together at each color change.

To twist the colors, bring the new color up from under the color just worked (Figure 1). This will "tack" the nonworking yarn against the back of the work and will prevent holes from forming on the front. When working intarsia, remember to keep your tension even and fluid to prevent puckers from forming at the color changes.

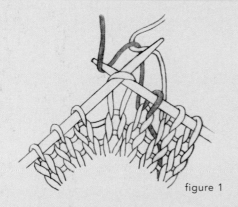

figure 1

Back

With CC1 and smaller straight needles, CO 78 (86, 94, 106) sts. Work in k2, p2 rib as foll:

ROW 1: (RS) *K2, p2; rep from * to last 2 sts, k2.

ROW 2: *P2, k2; rep from * to last 2 sts, p2.

Rep these 2 rows 9 more times—piece measures about 2½" (6.5 cm) from CO. Change to larger needles and MC. Beg with a RS row, work 4 (4, 4, 6) rows in St st (knit RS rows; purl WS rows) and *at the same time* inc 3 (1, 3, 0) st(s) in the first row—81 (87, 97, 106) sts.

SET-UP ROW: (RS) K1 (2, 1, 3) with MC, *work 15 sts according to Row 1 of Small Leaf chart (see page 30), k1 (2, 1, 2) with MC; rep from * 4 (4, 5, 5) more times, k0 (0, 0, 1) with MC.

Work as established through Row 16 of chart. Work 2 rows with MC. Beg and ending as indicated for your size, work Rows 1–6 of Triangles chart. Work 2 rows with CC3.

NEXT ROW: (RS) K1 (2, 7, 9) with CC3, work Row 1 of Beaver chart from left to right, k1 (3, 3, 5) with CC3, work Row 1 of Large Leaf chart, k1 (3, 3, 5) with CC3, work Row 1 of Beaver chart from right to left, k1 (2, 7, 10) with CC3.

Work as established through Row 27 of charts.

Work 2 rows with CC3. Beg with a WS row and beg and ending as indicated for your size, work Rows 1–6 of Triangles chart once more, reading from top to bottom to reverse patt. Change to MC and work even in St st until piece measures 15 (16, 17, 18)" (38 [40.5, 43, 45.5] cm) from CO, or desired length to underarm, ending with a WS row.

Shape Raglan

BO 4 sts at beg of next 2 rows—73 (79, 89, 98) sts rem.

DEC ROW: (RS) P1, k1, p1, ssk, knit to last 5 sts, k2tog, p1, k1, p1—2 sts dec'd.

NEXT ROW: Work sts as they appear.

Rep the last 2 rows 19 (21, 23, 27) more times—33 (35, 41, 42) sts rem. Place sts on holder.

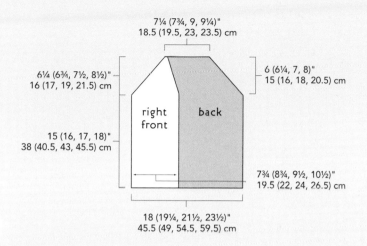

7¼ (7¾, 9, 9¼)"
18.5 (19.5, 23, 23.5) cm

6¼ (6¾, 7½, 8½)"
16 (17, 19, 21.5) cm

6 (6¼, 7, 8)"
15 (16, 18, 20.5) cm

right front

back

15 (16, 17, 18)"
38 (40.5, 43, 45.5) cm

7¾ (8¾, 9½, 10½)"
19.5 (22, 24, 26.5) cm

18 (19¼, 21½, 23½)"
45.5 (49, 54.5, 59.5) cm

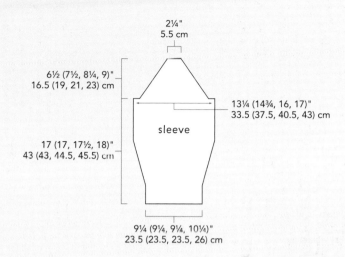

2¼"
5.5 cm

6½ (7½, 8¼, 9)"
16.5 (19, 21, 23) cm

13¼ (14¾, 16, 17)"
33.5 (37.5, 40.5, 43) cm

sleeve

17 (17, 17½, 18)"
43 (43, 44.5, 45.5) cm

9¼ (9¼, 9¼, 10¼)"
23.5 (23.5, 23.5, 26) cm

Left Front

With CC1 and smaller straight needles, CO 35 (39, 43, 47) sts. Work in k2, p2 rib as foll:

ROW 1: (RS) *K2, p2; rep from * to last 3 sts, k3.

ROW 2. P3, *k2, p2; rep from * to end.

Rep these 2 rows 9 more times—piece measures about 2½" (6.5 cm) from CO. Change to larger needles and MC. Beg with a RS row, work 4 (4, 4, 6) rows in St st.

SET-UP ROW: (RS) K2 (3, 5, 7) with MC, *work 15 sts according to Row 1 of Small Leaf chart, k1 (3, 3, 3) with MC; rep from * once more, k1 (0, 2, 4) with MC.

Work as established through Row 16 of chart. Work 2 rows with MC. Beg and ending as indicated for your size, work Rows 1–6 of Triangles chart. Work 2 rows with CC3.

NEXT ROW: (RS) K2 (4, 6, 8) with CC3, work 30 sts according to Row 1 of Beaver chart, reading from left to right, k3 (5, 7, 9) with CC3.

Work as established through Row 27 of chart. Work 2 rows with CC3. Beg with a WS row and beg and ending as indicated for your size, work Rows 1–6 of Triangles chart, reading from top to bottom to reverse patt. Change to MC and work even in St st until piece measures same length as back to underarm, ending with a WS row.

Shape Raglan

Note: Neck shaping is introduced as raglan decreases are worked; read all the way through the foll section before proceeding.

With RS facing, BO 4 sts, knit to end—31 (35, 39, 43) sts rem.

RAGLAN DEC ROW. (WS) Purl to last 5 sts, ssp (see Glossary), k1, p1, k1—1 st dec'd.

NEXT ROW: Work sts as they appear.

Rep the last 2 rows 19 (21, 23, 27) more times and *at the same time* beg on the first (second, second, second) raglan dec row, dec for neck as foll:

NECK DEC ROW: (WS) P1, p2tog, work to end of row—1 st dec'd at neck.

Beaver

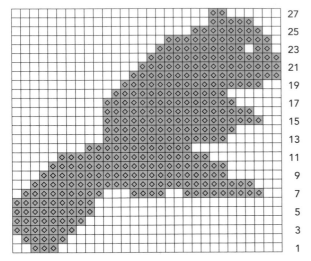

Large Leaf
Small Leaf

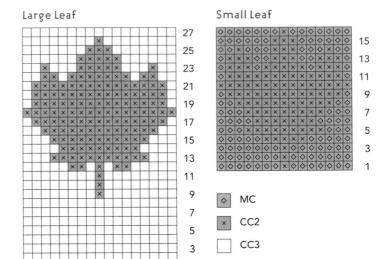

◇ MC

× CC2

☐ CC3

☐ pattern repeat

Triangles

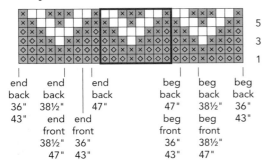

end	end	end	beg	beg	beg
back	back	back	back	back	back
36"	38½"	47"	47"	38½"	36"
43"	end	end	beg	beg	43"
	front	front	front	front	
	38½"	36"	36"	38½"	
	47"	43"	43"	47"	

Cont to work raglan decs as established, dec 1 st at neck edge in this manner every 6th row 5 (5, 7, 7) more times—5 (7, 7, 7) sts rem when all neck and raglan shaping is complete. Cont for your size as foll.

Size 36" (91.5 cm) only

NEXT ROW: (WS) P1, p3tog, p1—3 sts rem.

Knit 1 row. Place sts on holder.

Sizes 38½ (43, 47)" (98 [109, 119.5] cm) only

NEXT ROW: (WS) P1, p3tog, k1, p1, k1—5 sts rem.

NEXT ROW: Work sts as they appear.

NEXT ROW: P1, p3tog, p1—3 sts rem.

Knit 1 row. Place sts on holder.

Right Front

With CC1 and smaller straight needles, CO 35 (39, 43, 47) sts. Work in k2, p2 rib as foll:

ROW 1: (RS) K3, *p2, k2; rep from *.

ROW 2: *P2, k2; rep from * to last 3 sts, p3.

Rep these 2 rows 9 more times—piece measures about 2½" (6.5 cm) from CO. Change to larger needles and MC. Beg with a RS row, work 4 (4, 4, 6) rows in St st.

SET-UP ROW: (RS) K2 (3, 5, 7) with MC, *work 15 sts according to Row 1 of Small Leaf chart, k1 (3, 3, 3) with MC; rep from * once more, k1 (0, 2, 4) with MC.

Work as established through Row 16 of chart. Work 2 rows with MC. Beg and ending as indicated for your size, work Rows 1–6 of Triangles chart. Work 2 rows with CC3.

SET-UP ROW: (RS) K3 (5, 7, 9) with CC3, work 30 sts according to Row 1 of Beaver chart, reading from right to left, k2 (4, 6, 8) with CC3.

Work as established through Row 27 of chart. Work 2 rows

with CC3. Beg with a WS row and beg and ending as indicated for your size, work Rows 1–6 of Triangles chart, reading from top to bottom to reverse patt. Change to MC and work even in St st until piece measures same length as back to underarm, ending with a RS row.

Shape Raglan

Note: Neck shaping is introduced as raglan decreases are worked; read all the way through the foll section before proceeding.

With WS facing, BO 4 sts, purl to end—31 (35, 39, 43) sts rem.

RAGLAN DEC ROW: (RS) Knit to last 5 sts, k2tog, p1, k1, p1—1 st dec'd.

NEXT ROW: Work sts as they appear.

Rep the last 2 rows 19 (21, 23, 27) more times and *at the same time* beg on the first (second, second, second) raglan dec row, dec for neck as foll:

NECK DEC ROW: (RS) K1, ssk, work to end of row—1 st dec'd at neck.

Cont to work raglan decs as established, dec 1 st at neck edge in this manner every 6th row 5 (5, 7, 7) more times—5 (7, 7, 7) sts rem when all neck and raglan shaping is complete. Cont for your size as foll.

Size 36" (91.5 cm) only

NEXT ROW: (RS) K1, k3tog, k1—3 sts rem.

Purl 1 row. Place sts on holder.

Sizes 38½ (43, 47)" (98 [109, 119.5] cm) only

NEXT ROW: (RS) K1, k3tog, p1, k1, p1—5 sts rem.

NEXT ROW: Work sts as they appear.

NEXT ROW: K1, k3tog, k1—3 sts rem.

Purl 1 row. Place sts on holder.

Sleeves

With CC1 and smaller straight needles, CO 42 (42, 42, 46) sts. Work in k2, p2 rib as foll:

ROW 1: (RS) K2, *p2, k2; rep from *.

ROW 2: P2, *k2, p2; rep from *.

Rep these 2 rows 8 more times—18 rows total. Change to larger needles and MC. Beg with a knit row, work 6 rows in St st.

INC ROW: (RS) K1f&b (see Glossary), knit to last 2 sts, k1f&b, k1—2 sts inc'd.

Work 5 rows even in St st. Rep the last 6 rows 8 (11, 14, 14) more times—60 (66, 72, 76) sts. Work even in St st until piece measures 17 (17, 17½, 18)" (43 [43, 44.5, 45.5] cm) from CO or desired length to underarm, ending with a WS row.

Shape Raglan

BO 4 sts at beg of next 2 rows—52 (58, 64, 68) sts rem.

DEC ROW: (RS) P1, k1, p1, ssk, knit to last 5 sts, k2tog, p1, k1, p1—2 sts dec'd.

NEXT ROW: Work sts as they appear.

Rep the last 2 rows 20 (23, 26, 28) more times—10 sts rem. Place sts on holder.

Finishing

Block pieces to measurements. With yarn threaded on a tapestry needle, use the mattress st (see Glossary) to sew sleeve tops to front and back, aligning raglan decs and easing along raglan line. Sew sleeve and side seams.

Collar and Buttonband

With CC1, smaller cir needle, and RS facing, pick up and knit 70 (74, 79, 84) sts along center right front to neck shaping, place marker (pm), 30 (31, 35, 40) sts along neck shaping, k3 held right front sts, k10 held right sleeve sts, k33 (35, 41, 42) held back sts and *at the same time* dec 1 (1, 1, 2) st(s) evenly spaced, k10 held left sleeve sts, k3 held left front sts, pick up and knit 30 (31, 35, 40) sts along left neck shaping, pm, and 70 (74, 79, 84) sts along center left front—258 (270, 294, 314) sts total. Slip markers when you come to them.

ROW 1: (WS) *P2, k2; rep from * to last 2 sts, p2.

ROWS 2 AND 3: Work in rib as established.

Work short-rows (see page 70) for collar as foll:

SHORT-ROW 1: (RS) Work in rib as established to 4 sts before 2nd m, wrap next st, turn work.

SHORT-ROW 2: (WS) Work in rib as established to 4 sts before next m, wrap next st, turn work.

SHORT-ROW 3: Work in rib to 6 sts before last wrapped st, wrap next st, turn work.

Rep the last row 7 more times—5 wrapped sts each side.

NEXT 2 ROWS: Work to end of row, working wraps tog with wrapped sts.

Work 4 more rows in rib as established.

NEXT ROW: (RS; buttonhole row) K2, p2, *BO 2 sts, work 18 sts in patt; rep from * 3 more times, work to end in rib as established.

NEXT ROW: (WS; complete buttonholes) Work in rib as established and use the backward-loop method (see Glossary) to CO 2 sts over each BO gap on the previous row.

Work 6 more rows in rib as established.

With larger needle, loosely BO all sts in patt.

Sew buttons to left front opposite buttonholes. Weave in loose ends.

Whitby STOCKINGS

DESIGNED BY COURTNEY KELLEY

Named for a fishing village located on the north Yorkshire coast of England, these stockings remind me of paintings of "flither pickers" or "flithergirls" who sold limpets (small shellfish) to fishermen for bait near the turn of the twentieth century. Doubtless these young women wore their own knitted stockings, and while their stockings may have been knitted in undyed homespun, these Whitby Stockings feature stripes and small peerie patterns inspired by the Fair Isle sweaters of the northern islands. Knitted in earthy, muted colors similar to those attained through natural dyes, these extra-long stockings are designed to be shown off with a skirt or pair of cropped pants—just right for a cold wet day on the coast.

MATERIALS

yarn
Fingering weight (#1 Super Fine).

shown here: The Fibre Company Canopy Fingering (50% baby alpaca, 30% merino wool, 20% bamboo; 200 yd [183 m]/50 g): laguna (green; MC), 2 skeins; wild ginger (tan; CC1) and acai (coral; CC2), 1 skein each.

needles
leg and foot: size U.S. 2 (2.75 mm): set of 4 or 5 double-pointed (dpn).

ribbing: size U.S. 1 (2.25 mm): set of 4 or 5 dpn.

Adjust needle size if necessary to obtain the correct gauge.

notions
Markers (m); tapestry needle.

gauge
34 stitches and 40 rounds = 4" (10 cm) in stockinette stitch on larger needles, worked in rounds.

finished size
About 8" (20.5 cm) foot circumference and 10" (25.5 cm) foot length from back of heel to tip of toe. To fit woman's U.S. shoe sizes 8–9.

Note

> Except for the ribbing and one purl stitch, the socks are knitted in stockinette stitch. The purl stitch, which marks the beginning of the round, is at the center back of the leg.

Jogless Stripes

A downfall of knitting stripes in the round in that there is a jog in the color bands when one round transitions to the next. You can create a more even transition from one color to the next by working the first stitch together with the stitch in the row below on the second round of each new color.

STEP 1. Knit 1 round with the new color.

STEP 2. At the beginning of the next round, insert the right needle tip into the right leg (Figure 1) of the stitch in the row below the first stitch of the round (the old color) and place this stitch on the left-hand needle (Figure 2).

STEP 3. Knit this lifted stitch together with the first stitch of the round to raise the color of the previous round to the height of the new round.

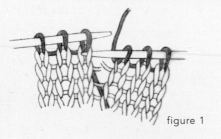

figure 1

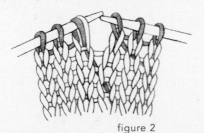

figure 2

Chart A

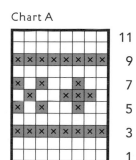

Chart B

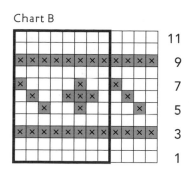

Chart C

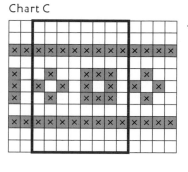

Chart D

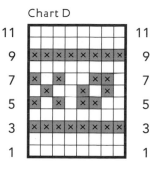

Chart E

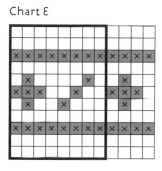

Chart F

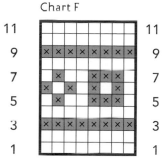

Chart G

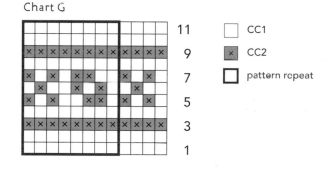

☐ CC1

☒ CC2

☐ pattern repeat

Leg

With MC and smaller dpn, CO 96 sts. Place marker (pm) and join for working in rnds, being careful not to twist sts. Work in p1, k1 rib until piece measures 2½" (6.5 cm) from CO. Change to larger dpn.

INC RND: Slip marker (sl m), p1, pm, M1 (see page 78), knit to end of rnd—97 sts.

Always purling the first st of the rnd, work rem 96 sts in St st for 12 rnds

Working the purl st in the background color, cont as foll:

Work Rows 1–11 of Chart A between m. Change to MC and knit 3 rnds.

DEC RND: P1, k1, ssk, knit to 3 sts before m, k2tog, k1—2 sts dec'd.

Knit 4 rnds. Rep dec rnd—93 sts rem. Knit 3 rnds—piece measures about 6" (15 cm) from CO.

Work Rows 1–11 of Chart B between m as before. Change to MC and knit 3 rnds. Rep dec rnd—91 sts rem. Knit 2 rnds.

Rep dec rnd—89 sts rem. Knit 2 rnds. Rep dec rnd—87 sts rem. Knit 2 rnds—piece measures about 8½" (21.5 cm) from CO.

Work Rows 1–11 of Chart C between m as before. Change to MC and knit 3 rnds. Rep dec rnd—85 sts rem. Knit 2 rnds. Rep dec rnd—83 sts rem. Knit 2 rnds. Rep dec rnd—81 sts rem. Knit 2 rnds—piece measures about 10¾" (27.5 cm) from CO.

Work Rows 1–11 of Chart D between m as before. Change to MC and knit 3 rnds. Rep dec rnd—79 sts rem. Knit 4 rnds. Rep dec rnd—77 sts rem. Knit 3 rnds—piece measures about 13" (33 cm) from CO.

Work Rows 1–11 of Chart E between m as before. Change to MC and knit 3 rnds. Rep dec rnd—75 sts rem. Knit 4 rnds. Rep dec rnd—73 sts rem. Knit 3 rnds—piece measures about 15¼" (38.5 cm) from CO.

Work Rows 1–11 of Chart F between m as before. Change to MC and knit 3 rnds. Rep dec rnd—71 sts rem. Knit 4 rnds. Rep dec rnd—69 sts rem. Knit 3 rnds—piece measures about 17½" (44.5 cm) from CO.

Work Rows 1–11 of Chart G between m as before. Change to MC and knit 5 rnds.

NEXT RND: Sl m, k1, remove m, k2tog, knit to last 17 sts, change to CC2, knit to end of rnd—68 sts rem; piece measures about 19¼" (49 cm) from CO. Remove m.

Heel

Divide for heel as foll: K17, turn work. Place 34 CC2 sts onto one needle for heel; rem 34 sts will be worked later for instep.

Heel Flap

Work 34 heel sts back and forth in rows as foll:

ROW 1: (WS) Sl 1, p33.

ROW 2: (RS) Sl 1, k33.

Rep these 2 rows 15 more times, then work Row 1 once more—33 rows total.

Shape Heel

Work short-rows as foll:

ROW 1: (RS) Sl 1, k21, ssk, turn work.

ROW 2: (WS) Sl 1, p10, p2tog, turn work.

ROW 3: Sl 1, k10, ssk, turn work.

Rep Rows 2 and 3 nine more times, then work Row 2 once more—12 heel sts rem.

Gussets

JOINING RND: Sl 1, knit to end of heel sts with CC2, change to MC and pick up and knit 17 sts along selvedge edge of heel flap, pm, k34 held instep sts, pm, pick up and knit 17 sts along other selvedge edge of heel flap, knit the first 6 heel sts again, pm to denote beg of rnd—80 sts total.

RND 1: Knit to 3 sts before m, k2tog, k1, k34 instep sts, k1, ssk, knit to end of rnd—2 sts dec'd.

RND 2: Knit.

Rep these 2 rnds 5 more times—68 sts rem.

Foot

With MC, work even until piece measures 7½" (19 cm) from back of heel, or 2½" (6.5 cm) less than desired finished length.

Toe

Change to CC2 and dec as foll:

RND 1: Knit to 3 sts before m, k2tog, k2, ssk, knit to 3 sts before m, k2tog, k2, ssk, knit to end of rnd—4 sts dec'd.

RND 2: Knit.

Rep these 2 rnds 11 more times—20 sts rem. Knit to first m. Cut yarn, leaving a 10" (25.5 cm) tail.

Finishing

Place 10 sts between m onto one needle and 10 rem sts onto another needle. Thread tail on a tapestry needle and use the Kitchener st (see Glossary) to graft rem sts tog. Weave in loose ends. Block lightly.

Cady TWISTED-STITCH MITTENS

DESIGNED BY KATE GAGNON OSBORN

The two-end knitting technique, known as twined knitting or *tvåändsstickning*, is created when two strands of the same color are alternated stitch by stitch. Common theory is that twined knitting originated in Sweden, perhaps as far back as 1680, to produce a strong, warm fabric that could withstand hard wear during the long winters. These mittens are worked in a variation of the traditional technique in which the two strands are worked Fair Isle fashion with one yarn always carried on top of the other in the back of the work. Beginning with a lined picot cuff, these mittens are decorated with knit and purl stitches to provide subtle texture to the design.

MATERIALS

yarn
Fingering weight (#1 Super Fine).

shown here: The Fibre Company Canopy Fingering (50% baby alpaca, 30% merino wool, 20% bamboo; 200 yd [183 m]/50 g): chiclet tree, 2 skeins.

needles
Size U.S. 1½ (2.5 mm): set of 4 or 5 double-pointed (dpn).

Adjust needle size if necessary to obtain the correct gauge.

notions
Smooth cotton waste yarn for provisional cast-on; markers (m); stitch holder; tapestry needle; six ³⁄₁₆" (5 mm) pearl shank buttons.

gauge
38 stitches and 34 rounds = 4" (10 cm) in charted hand pattern, worked in rounds.

finished size
About 6¼" (16 cm) hand circumference and 11½" (29 cm) long from cuff to tip of finger. These mittens are designed for a snug fit for a medium-size woman's hand.

Technique Tips

These mittens use several specific techniques, all of which can be facilitated with a few tips.

Provisional Cast-On

Use a waste yarn of comparable gauge but smooth texture. Cotton works well for this as it does not stick to the working yarn or to itself.

Single-Color Latvian Braid

When one works a Latvian braid, the yarns get twisted around one another on the first round, then untwisted on the following round. To make this easier, loosen enough yarn from each ball to work a full round before beginning.

Knitting the Provisional Cast-On Stitches Together with the Cuff

Because the provisional cast on is folded to the inside of the work, you may find it fussy to put all of the stitches on another set of needles. To avoid this, "unzip" 5 to 10 stitches at a time, place them on a spare needle, and work them together with the live stitches.

Stranded Knitting

To facilitate working stranded knitting, designate one end to be carried on top of the other. Maintain even tension on the stranded yarn at the back of the work (or in the front when working stitch patterns). When working the purled cuff pattern, make sure to bring the yarn to the back of the work before bringing the next yarn to the front.

Cuff

With waste yarn (see box at left) and using a provisional method (see Glossary), CO 56 sts. Divide sts as evenly as possible on 3 or 4 dpn. Place marker (pm) and join for working in rnds, being careful not to twist sts. With MC, knit 21 rnds—piece measures about 1¾" (4.5 cm) from CO.

PICOT RND: *K2tog, yo; rep from *.

Knit 3 rnds.

INC RND: *K14, M1 (see page 78); rep from *—60 sts.

Braid

RND 1: (see box at left) Bring yarn to front of work and join second strand of MC (designated MC2) and holding yarn in front, *p1 MC, cross MC2 over MC strand just worked, p1 MC2, cross MC over MC2 strand just worked; rep from *.

Hand and Thumb

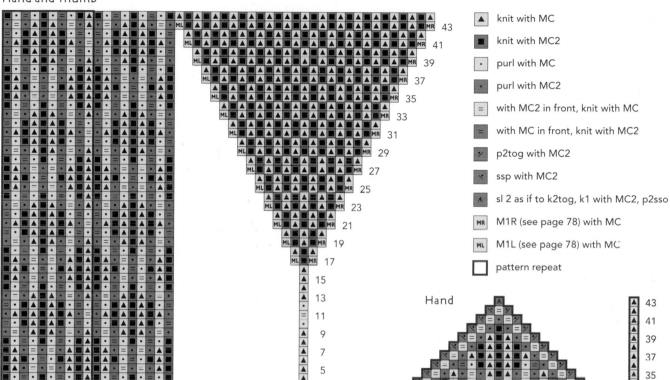

43
41
39
37
35
33
31
29
27
25
23
21
19
17
15
13
11
9
7
5
3
1

▲	knit with MC
■	knit with MC2
·	purl with MC
●	purl with MC2
=	with MC2 in front, knit with MC
—	with MC in front, knit with MC2
↘	p2tog with MC2
↙	ssp with MC2
⋀	sl 2 as if to k2tog, k1 with MC2, p2sso
MR	M1R (see page 78) with MC
ML	M1L (see page 78) with MC
☐	pattern repeat

Hand

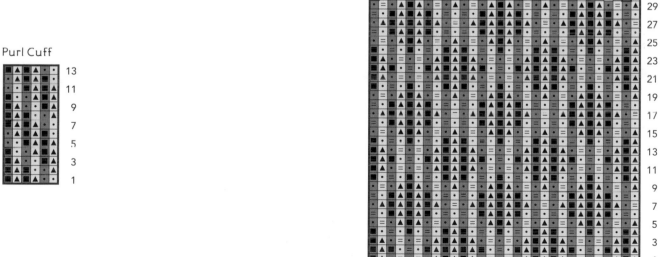

43
41
39
37
35
33
31
29
27
25
23
21
19
17
15
13
11
9
7
5
3
1

Purl Cuff

13
11
9
7
5
3
1

RND 2: Beg with MC, work as for Rnd 1, but cross the next strand to be worked *under* the strand just worked.

Work Rnds 1–13 of Purl Cuff chart. Rep Rnds 1 and 2 of Braid.

Hem

With RS facing and using MC only, fold work along picot rnd, remove waste yarn from provisional CO and transfer exposed sts to spare needle (see page 42), *[knit first st on needle tog with first exposed CO st] 14 times, k1; rep from *.

Hand

Alternating 1 st from each ball for stranded knitting as shown on chart (see page 43), work Rnds 1–44 of Hand and Thumb chart—88 sts. Place 29 thumb sts on waste yarn holder. Using the backward-loop method (see Glossary), CO 1 st with MC (counts as first st of rnd)—60 sts. Work Rnds 1–43 of Hand chart—4 sts rem. Cut yarns, leaving 6" (15 cm) tails. Thread tails on tapestry needle, draw through rem sts, pull tight to close hole and secure on WS.

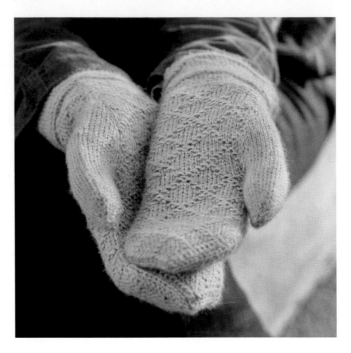

Thumb

Distribute 29 held thumb sts evenly on 3 or 4 dpn. Join 2 balls of yarn and pick up and knit 1 st in the gap between the thumb and hand—30 sts. Pm and join for working in rnds. Work in St st stranded knitting until thumb measures about 1¼" (3.2 cm), or ¾" (2 cm) less than desired finished length.

DEC RND 1: *K4, k2tog; rep from *—25 sts rem.

DEC RND 2: *K3, k2tog; rep from *—20 sts rem.

DEC RND 3: *K2, k2tog; rep from *—15 sts rem.

DEC RND 4: *K1, k2tog; rep from *—10 sts rem.

DEC RND 5: *K2tog; rep from *—5 sts rem.

Cut yarns, leaving 6" (15 cm) tails. Thread tails on tapestry needle, draw through rem sts, pull tight to close hole and secure on WS.

Finishing

Weave in loose ends. Sew three buttons on each cuff as desired. Block to measurements.

Margarethe LACE SHAWL

DESIGNED BY KATE GAGNON OSBORN

There are two characteristics that distinguish Faroese shawls from other triangular lace shawls—a center gore that divides two triangular sides and shoulder shaping that provides a unique butterfly-wing shape for a better fit. Typically, Faroese shawls are knitted in domestic sheep's wool in natural colors, employing garter stitch for the main portion of the body. This updated take on tradition is knitted in a luxurious and drapey blend of alpaca, silk, camel, and cashmere for next-to-the-skin softness and incredible warmth. It begins with a garter edge, transitioning into a classic lace pattern that flanks a center lace panel. The body is worked in stockinette stitch with garter edges and the shoulders are shaped with double decreases integrated along the neck edge, rather than across the main body portion.

MATERIALS

yarn
Sportweight (#2 Fine).

shown here: The Fibre Company Road to China Light (65% baby alpaca, 15% silk, 10% camel, 10% cashmere; 159 yd [145 m]/50 g): carnelian, 5 (7) skeins.

needles
body: size U.S. 5 (3.75 mm): 36" (90 cm) circular (cir).

border: size U.S. 4 (3.5 mm): 36" (90 cm) cir.

Adjust needle size if necessary to obtain the correct gauge.

notions
Markers (m); tapestry needle.

gauge
22 stitches and 32 rows = 4" (10 cm) in stockinette stitch on larger needle, after blocking.

finished size
About 56 (66)" (142 [167.5] cm) wide at top and 27 (32)" (68.5 [81.5] cm) long, after blocking. Shawl shown in larger size.

Note

> The shawl is shaped by working additional decreases (not paired with yarnover increases) at the beginning, at each side of the center panel, and at the end of every right-side row (4 decreases total). Note that the stitch count in the main pattern repeat is always 17 stitches.

Reading Lace Charts

At first glance, many knitters find charts to be a daunting—even project-stopping—task. But charts provide a succinct way to tell the knitter what to do, and better yet, in contrast to written instructions, provide a map for exactly how the knitting should look.

Once you've mastered a basic understanding of the symbols, you'll find charts to be an easy way to read lace patterns. In general, charts are always read in the same direction as you knit. Right-side rows are read from right to left; wrong-side rows are read from left to right. The symbols represent the action made on that row, as viewed from the right side of the knitting, not what is already on the needles.

The chart below is a simple 3-stitch pattern repeat that is worked over 4 rows. Written out, the instructions would read:

ROW 1: (RS) *K1, yo, k2tog; rep from * to last st, k1.

ROW 2: (WS) Purl.

ROWS 3 AND 4: Rep Rows 1 and 2.

Broken down into motifs, the "yo, k2tog" pairings are aligned vertically. Although k2tog is actually worked over two stitches, the symbol only occupies one box because this action results in one stitch decreased, leaving just one stitch on the needle. Similarly, a yarnover occupies one box because it produces one new stitch. When the number of yarnovers matches the number of decreases, there is no change to the stitch count. If, as you knit this pattern, the yarnovers don't align vertically or the number of stitches changes from row to row, you'll know you've made a mistake.

Shawl

With larger needle, CO 347 (411) sts. Do not join.

Change to smaller needle and knit 8 rows, beg with a WS row—4 garter ridges.

Border

SET-UP ROW: (WS) K5, place marker (pm), k160 (192), pm, k17, pm, k160 (192), pm, k5.

Slipping markers every row and working the sts in the red rep boxes 8 (10) times, work Rows 1–46 of Lace Border chart—287 (351) sts rem; piece measures about 6¼" (16 cm) from CO.

Body

Change to larger needle.

Note: Beg with Row 7 of Center Lace Panel chart.

DEC ROW: (RS) K5, k2tog, knit to 2 sts before next m, ssk, work 17 sts according to Center Lace Panel chart, k2tog, knit to 2 sts before next m, ssk, k5—4 sts dec'd.

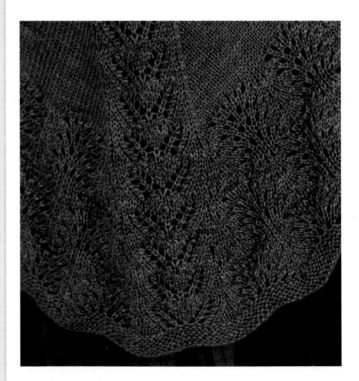

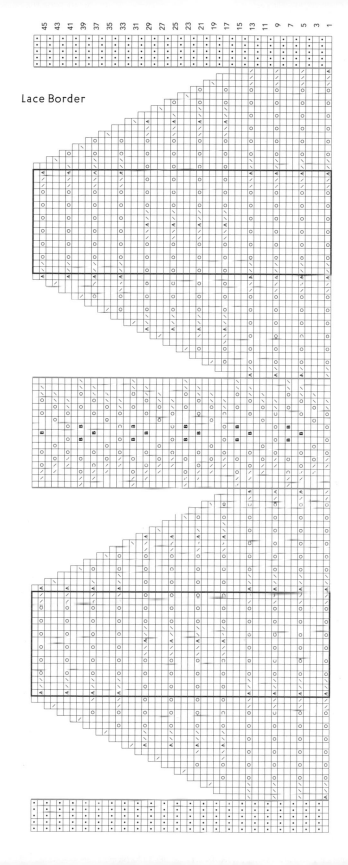

Lace Border

Center Lace Panel

\	\	O	O		B		B			O		O	/	/	7
\	\	O	O			B			O		O	/	/		5
	\	\	O	O					O		O	/	/		3
		\	\	O	O			O		O	/	/			1

☐ k on RS; p on WS

· p on RS; k on WS

O yo

∕ k2tog

∖ ssk

⋀ sl 2 as if to k2tog, k1, p2sso

B (k1, yo, k1) in same st, turn; p3, turn; sl 2 as if to k2tog, k1, p2sso

▢ pattern repeat

❘ marker position

MARGARETHE SHAWL49

NEXT ROW: K5, purl to last 5 sts, k5.

Rep the last 2 rows 30 (37) more times—163 (199) sts rem; piece measures about 16¾ (19¼)" (42.5 [49] cm) from CO.

Decrease for Shoulders

ROW 1: K5, k3tog, knit to 2 sts before next m, ssk, work 17 sts according to Center Lace Panel chart as established, k2tog, knit to 3 sts before next m, sl 2 as if to k2tog, k1, p2sso, k5—6 sts dec'd.

ROW 2: K5, purl to last 5 sts, k5.

ROWS 3, 5, AND 7: K5, k2tog, knit to 2 sts before next m, ssk, work 17 sts according to Center Lace Panel chart, k2tog, knit to 2 sts before next m, ssk, k5—4 sts dec'd each row.

ROWS 4, 6, AND 8: K5, purl to last 5 sts, k5.

Rep these 8 rows 6 (8) more times—37 sts rem; piece measures about 25½ (30½)" (65 [77.5] cm) from CO.

Shape Neck

ROW 1: K5, k2tog, k1, ssk, work 17 sts in patt as established, k2tog, k1, ssk, k5—33 sts rem.

ROW 2: K5, purl to last 5 sts, k5.

ROW 3: K5, remove m, sl 2 as if to k2tog, k1, p2sso, remove m, work 17 sts in patt as established, remove m, sl 2 as if to k2tog, k1, p2sso, remove m, k5—29 sts rem.

ROW 4: K5, purl to last 5 sts, k5.

Join Garter-Stitch Edging To Top of Lace Panel

Work short-rows as foll:

ROW 1: (RS) K4, ssk, turn work—1 st dec'd.

ROW 2: (WS) K5, turn work.

Rep these 2 rows 16 more times—12 sts rem.

NEXT ROW: (RS) K4, sl 2 as if to k2tog, k1, p2sso, turn work—10 sts rem.

NEXT ROW: (WS) K5.

Finishing

Place 5 sts each on 2 needles and hold the needles with RS facing tog. Use the three-needle method (see Glossary) to BO the sts tog. Weave in loose ends.

Soak in warm water and wool wash. Squeeze out excess water, pin flat to measurements, and allow to air-dry completely.

VINTAGE FEMININE

AS WINTER NEARS AN END, sunny afternoons begin and end with cool mornings and evenings. Tulips and daffodils slowly arise from their winter hibernation and wash the once bare landscape with bright greens, pinks, and purples to announce the arrival of spring. Outdoor activities commence—long walks to town, bike rides to the open-air market to purchase early harvests, and evening visits with friends. Heavy winter coats are stored away and lighter layers take their place to be easily removed as the sun warms the earth and then gratefully replaced as it sets.

All of the garments and accessories in this collection incorporate vintage-inspired soft hues, flowery motifs, and feminine elements to express the feeling of renewal brought by spring. Lace, embroidery, cables, and Fair Isle patterns demonstrate attention to details and vintage touches. Functional elements designed to flatter are the main focus of these projects.

Designed to look like heirlooms passed down from generations—or the best thrift store finds of the decade—these pieces require just a bit of the knitter's concentration and effort. The tailored quality and delicate stitches pay homage to an age when all craftsmen took care to create well-made lasting items. The end result—a fitted lightweight cardigan or a fully fashioned beret, for example—is well worth every stitch.

Ginger LACE CARDIGAN

DESIGNED BY COURTNEY KELLEY

I love the look of vintage allover lace cardigans from the 1950s and 1960s, but the instructions often seem so vague. In those days, many patterns provided just a stitch repeat and instructions to "keep in pattern" while working armhole, neck, and sleeve shaping instead of writing out row-by-row instructions. It struck me one day that if I charted the increases and decreases just as I would for a shawl, I'd be able to visualize how the shaping affects the lace pattern. Suddenly, all those lace cardigans became a lot less daunting. Once you're accustomed to following the charts, you'll find the simple style of this pretty cardigan to be a wardrobe staple.

MATERIALS

yarn
Sportweight (#2 Fine).

shown here: The Fibre Company Road to China Light (65% baby alpaca, 15% silk, 10% cashmere, 10% camel; 159 yd [145 m]/50 g): autumn jasper (tan), 9 (11, 12) skeins.

needles
body and sleeves: size 4 (3.5 mm): 32" (80 cm) circular (cir).

hems and cuffs: size 3 (3.25 mm): 24" (60 cm) cir.

Adjust needle size if necessary to obtain the correct gauge.

notions
Markers (m); stitch holders or waste yarn; tapestry needle; ten (eleven, eleven) ⅝" (1.5 cm) buttons.

gauge
24 stitches and 36 rows = 4" (10 cm) in lace pattern on larger needle, lightly steamed.

finished size
About 36½ (43, 49½)" (92.5 [109, 125.5] cm) bust circumference.
Sweater shown measures 36½" (92.5 cm), buttoned.

Note

> When working raglan shaping on the fronts for the first size, if there are not enough stitches to work the "knit 2," knit either 1 or 0 stitch instead.

Stitch Guide

Seed Stitch (multiple of 2 sts + 1)

ALL ROWS: *K1, p1; rep from * to last st, k1.

Shaping in Lace Patterns

It took me years of knitting lace shawls before I began to think of garments as good candidates for lace patterns. Many sweaters with allover lace patterns have drop-shoulder construction, which certainly makes the knitting easy, but it doesn't have the flattering fit I like. Some garments are worked with a vertical band of stockinette stitch at the side seams positioned so that it doesn't interfere with the armhole shaping. Recently, as I designed a lace shawl by decreasing every other row to create a triangular shape, I realized that the same method could be used to shape the armhole of a raglan sweater.

I began the Ginger Lace Cardigan by charting multiple repeats of the lace pattern on a large sheet of graph paper and outlining the pattern repeat in a contrasting color. Based on my stitch and row gauge, I calculated the number of stitches that needed to be decreased over the number of rows in the armhole. Then, with my eraser handy, I began to "cut" into the pattern in a stairstep fashion—remove one stitch at each edge, work one row plain, remove one stitch, work one row plain, and so on until I removed the necessary number of stitches (Figure 1). In order to ensure that I hadn't removed a decrease without removing its accompanying increase (and vice versa), I erased all of the symbols that represented partial lace pattern repeats. This left only whole repeats and the knowledge that the shaping wouldn't interfere with the lace pattern. Then, I carefully replaced lace symbols to create partial motifs at the edges, always including a decrease for every increase (and vice versa), so that the partial motifs were mirror images on each side of the piece, just as if I were designing a triangular shawl with a center row of decreases. The same method can be used to add the lace pattern into new stitches that are increased, to shape a sleeve, for example (Figure 2). After that, I identified the repeat of the decreases so that I could follow just that part of the chart. I approach shaping this way from a purely visual standpoint—if I plot all the knitting on paper before I cast on stitches, I'm confident the project will be a success. Experiment! It's all worth the effort, even if it's only on pencil and paper.

Sidebar Raglan Decreases (Figure 1)

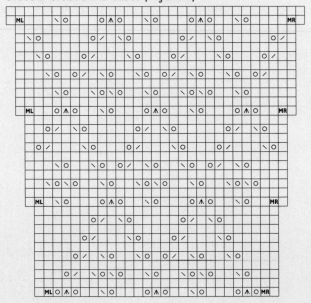

□	k on RS; p on WS
○	yo
╱	k2tog
╲	ssk
⋀	sl 2 as if to k2tog, k1, p2sso
MR	M1R (see page 78)
ML	M1L (see page 78)

Sidebar Sleeve Increases (Figure 2)

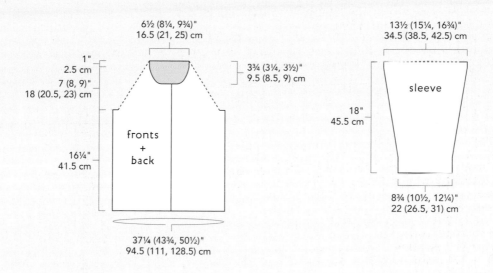

6½ (8¼, 9¾)"
16.5 (21, 25) cm

1"
2.5 cm

7 (8, 9)"
18 (20.5, 23) cm

3¾ (3¼, 3½)"
9.5 (8.5, 9) cm

fronts
+
back

16¼"
41.5 cm

37¼ (43¾, 50½)"
94.5 (111, 128.5) cm

13½ (15¼, 16¾)"
34.5 (38.5, 42.5) cm

sleeve

18"
45.5 cm

8¾ (10½, 12¼)"
22 (26.5, 31) cm

Body

With smaller needle, CO 223 (263, 303) sts. Do not join. Work in seed st (see Stitch Guide) for 9 rows.

BUTTONHOLE ROW: (RS) K1, p1, k2tog, yo, work in seed st as established to end of row.

Work 14 more rows in seed st. Change to larger needle.

SET-UP ROW 1: (WS) Work 6 sts in seed st as established, place marker (pm), purl to last 6 sts, pm, work to end in seed st as established.

SET-UP ROW 2: (RS) Work 6 sts in seed st, slip marker (sl m), work Row 1 of Diamond Trellis chart (see page 58) to last 6 sts, sl m, work to end in seed st.

Cont in patt as established, work Rows 1–20 of chart 6 times, then work Rows 1–7 once more—piece measures about 16¼" (41.5 cm) from CO. *At the same time* work buttonhole on first 6 sts of every Row 9 of chart 8 (9, 9) times as foll: K1, p1, k2tog, yo, k1, p1, work to end as established.

Note: Yoke beg before buttonholes end.

Divide for Yoke

(WS: Row 8 of chart) Work 6 sts in seed st for buttonband, p46 (56, 66) for left front, BO 10 sts for left armhole, purl until there are 99 (119, 139) sts on needle for back, BO 10 sts for right armhole, purl until there are 46 (56, 66) sts for right front, work 6 sts in seed st for buttonhole band—52 (62, 72) sts rem for each front, 99 (119, 139) sts rem for back. Place all sts on holders.

Sleeves

With smaller needle, CO 53 (63, 73) sts. Do not join. Work in seed st for 18 rows. Change to larger needle. Purl 1 (WS) row.

SET-UP ROW: (RS) K1, work Row 1 of Diamond Trellis chart to last st, k1.

Work 7 more rows in patt, working the first and last st of every row in St st (knit on RS; purl on WS).

INC ROW: (RS; Row 9 of chart) K1, M1R (see page 78), work in patt to last st, M1L (see page 78), k1—2 sts inc'd.

Diamond Trellis

	k on RS; p on WS
o	yo
╱	k2tog
╲	ssk
⋀	sl 2 as if to k2tog, k1, p2sso
☐	pattern repeat

Rep inc row every 10th row (Rows 19 and 9 of chart) 13 more times, working new sts into patt—81 (91, 101) sts. Work through Row 7 of chart.

NEXT ROW: (WS; Row 8 of chart) BO 5 sts, work in patt to last 5 sts, BO 5 sts—71 (81, 91) sts rem. Place sts on holder.

Yoke

With larger cir needle, join body and sleeves as foll:

JOINING RND: (Row 9 of chart) For right front, work button-hole over 6 seed sts, yo, ssk, k2, yo, [sl 2, k1, p2sso, yo, k3, yo, ssk, k2, yo] 3 (4, 5) times, sl 2, k1, p2sso, yo, k3, yo, ssk, k4, pm; for right sleeve, k5, yo, ssk, k2, yo, [sl 2, k1, p2sso, yo, k3, yo, ssk, k2, yo] 5 (6, 7) times, sl 2, k1, p2sso, yo, k3, yo, ssk, k4, pm; for back, k4, yo, ssk, k2, yo, [sl 2, k1, p2sso, yo, k3, yo, ssk, k2, yo] 8 (10, 12) times, sl 2, k1, p2sso, yo, k3, yo, ssk, k3, pm; for left sleeve, k5, yo, ssk, k2, yo, [sl 2, k1, p2sso, yo, k3, yo, ssk, k2, yo] 5 (6, 7) times, sl 2, k1, p2sso, yo, k3, yo, ssk, k4, pm; for left front, k4, k2tog, yo, k3, yo, [sl 2, k1, p2sso, yo, k3, yo, ssk, k2, yo] 3 (4, 5) times, sl 2, k1, p2sso, yo, k2, k2tog, yo, work rem 6 sts in seed st—345 (405, 465) sts total; 52 (62, 72) sts for each front, 99 (119, 139) sts for back, 71 (81, 91) sts for each sleeve.

Keeping 4 sts each side of each m in St st, work 1 (WS) row.

RAGLAN DEC ROW: (RS) *Work in patt to 5 sts before m (see Notes), k2, k2tog, k1, sl m, k1, ssk, k2; rep from * 3 more times, work in patt to end—8 sts dec'd.

Rep the last 2 rows 29 (34, 39) more times, working button-holes as established, and *at the same time* beg on 19th (26th, 29th) dec row of yoke, shape neck as foll.

Neck

Place 6 band sts at each end of needle on holders; break yarn and rejoin at beg of RS row (after held sts). Cont with raglan shaping, BO 2 sts at beg of next 2 rows, then BO 3 sts at beg of foll 2 (4, 4) rows, then BO 2 sts at beg of foll 6 (2, 2) rows.

Dec 1 st at each neck edge every RS row 3 (2, 2) times—65 (89, 109) sts rem when all raglan and neck shaping is complete; 2 (9, 14) sts for each front, 39 (49, 59) sts for back, 11 sts for each sleeve. Work 1 (WS) row. Do not BO. Break yarn.

Finishing

Neckband

With RS facing and smaller needle, work 6 held band sts in seed st, pick up and knit 25 (21, 22) sts along right front neck edge; beg with a purl (knit, purl) st, work 65 (89, 109) neck sts in seed st, pick up and knit 25 (21, 22) sts along left front neck edge, work 6 held band sts in seed st—127 (143, 165) sts total. Work 5 rows even in seed st, ending with a WS row.

NEXT ROW: (RS) Work buttonhole on first 6 sts, work to end in seed st.

Work 3 rows even in seed st. BO all sts in patt.

Sew buttons to left front band opposite buttonholes. With yarn threaded on a tapestry needle, use the mattress st (see Glossary) to sew sleeve and underarm seams. Weave in loose ends. Steam lightly to block.

Yvette ROOSITUD HAT

DESIGNED BY KATE GAGNON OSBORN

Roositud is an Estonian inlay technique in which a contrasting color is wrapped back and forth between the front and back of the fabric as it is knitted, resulting in a geometric pattern that looks similar to embroidery. The roositud technique allows the knitter freedom to place a motif anywhere and to use as many colors as desired. Three colors are used to create detailed patterning in this beret, and the pattern yarns are doubled for a fuller overall effect. Traditionally, roositud inlay was used only on mittens and stockings, but the technique is worked as a graphic motif on one side of this beret for an update on tradition.

MATERIALS

yarn
Sportweight (#2 Fine).

shown here: The Fibre Company Road to China Light (65% baby alpaca, 15% silk, 10% camel, 10% cashmere; 159 yd [145 m]/50 g): riverstone (beige; MC), 2 skeins; peridot (green; CC1), hematite (gray; CC2), and carnelian (red; CC3), 1 skein each.

needles
hat: size U.S. 3 (3.25 mm): 16" (40 cm) circular (cir) and set of 4 or 5 double pointed (dpn).

ribbing: size U.S. 1 (2.25 mm): 16" (40 cm) cir.

Adjust needle size if necessary to obtain the correct gauge.

notions
Markers (m); tapestry needle.

gauge
26 stitches and 33 rounds = 4" (10 cm) in stockinette stitch on larger needles, worked in rounds.

finished size
About 19" (48.5 cm) in circumference at brim, 25¾" (65.5 cm) circumference at widest point, and 8¼" (21 cm) tall.

Roositud Inlay

This inlay technique is worked by following a charted pattern in a series of two-round sequences.

RND 1: Work the first round according to the charted pattern, moving the inlay yarn forward and back between the needles as specified, making sure not to pull the yarn too tightly (Figure 1).

RND 2:

STEP 1. Knit to the beginning of the inlay pattern.

STEP 2. Lift the inlay yarn from back to front over the top of the left-hand needle, then place it front to back between the needles where you are working (Figure 2), leaving a loose loop of inlay yarn.

STEP 3. At the end of the first group of inlay sts, place the left side of the loop of yarn between the needles to the back (Figure 3), then bring the loop to the front and back as specified by the chart for each following group of inlay stitches (Figure 4). After all inlay stitches have been worked, tug on the loose end of the inlay loop to tighten the stitches (Figure 5). The inlay yarn is now in position to work the next round.

Repeat these 2 rounds to complete the charted pattern.

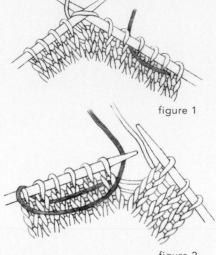

figure 1

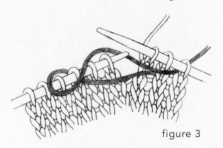

figure 2

figure 3

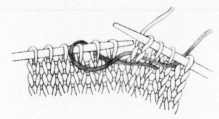

figure 4

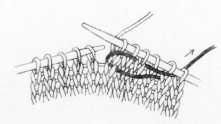

figure 5

Hat

With MC, larger cir needle, and using a provisional method (see Glossary), CO 62 sts. Do not join. Purl 1 (WS) row, knit 1 row, then purl 1 row. Remove waste yarn from provisional CO and carefully place 62 exposed sts onto smaller needle. Hold needles parallel with larger needle in front and WS of fabric facing tog.

JOINING ROW: (RS) With smaller needle, *k1 from front needle, p1 from back needle; rep from *—124 sts.

Cont with smaller cir needle, place marker (pm), and join for working in rnds, being careful not to twist sts. Work in k1, p1 rib until piece measures 1½" (3.8 cm) from CO.

INC RND: *K2, M1 (see page 78), [k3, M1] 5 times, k2, M1, [k3, M1] 4 times; rep from *—168 sts.

Change to larger cir needle. Work roositud inlay (see sidebar at left) as foll:

NEXT RND: K14, pm for beg of chart, work 35 sts according to Rnd 1 of Roositud chart, pm for end of chart, knit to end.

Cont in patt through Rnd 35 of chart.

Roositud

+	MC
◿	roositud inlay with 2 strands CC1
▲	roositud inlay with 2 strands CC2
=	roositud inlay with 2 strands CC3
╱	k2tog with MC
╲	ssk with MC
‖	marker position

Shape Crown

Note: You will cont working Roositud chart through Rnd 49, then work all sts with MC; crown shaping is also shown on chart for clarity.

SET-UP RND: (Rnd 36 of chart) *Work 21 sts, pm for shaping; rep from * 7 more times.

DEC RND: *Ssk, work to 2 sts before shaping m, k2tog; rep from *—16 sts dec'd.

Work 2 rnds even. Rep last 3 rnds once more—136 sts rem. Rep dec rnd. Work 1 rnd even. Rep last 2 rnds 5 more times, then work dec rnd once more—24 sts rem.

NEXT RND: [Sl 2 as if to k2tog, k1, p2sso] 8 times—8 sts rem.

Cut yarn, leaving an 8" (20.5 cm) tail. Thread tail on a tapestry needle, draw through rem sts two or three times, pull tight to close hole, and fasten off on WS.

Finishing

Weave in all MC loose ends. Cut inlay strands to about 5" (12.5 cm) but do not weave in these ends. Soak hat in warm water and wool wash and lay flat to dry. When dry, adjust inlay yarns as necessary for even tension, then weave in the ends.

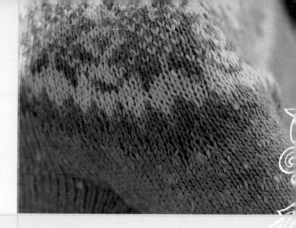

Adelaide
YOKE PULLOVER

DESIGNED BY KATE GAGNON OSBORN

Icelandic yoke sweaters were first introduced to the public in the mid-twentieth century, inspired by a variety of knitting techniques and cultures that included the Bohus yoke pullovers introduced by Anna-Lisa Mannheimer Lunn, classic Norwegian lice-stitch sweaters, and intricate beaded collars of the Greenland National Costume. Although a young technique relative to the lengthy history of knitting, this style of sweater is a true classic design that is easily identifiable among knitters. The Adelaide pullover is directly inspired by Icelandic sweaters but has been updated with a longer, closer fit, waist shaping, and short-rows prior to the Fair Isle patterning for a good fit and comfortable neckline. Ultrafeminine soft colors are utilized in lieu of traditional natural sheep colors for an additional twist on tradition.

finished size
About 31½ (35½, 40½, 44½, 48½, 52½)" (80 [90, 103, 113, 123, 133.5] cm) bust circumference. Sweater is designed for a close fit with zero ease. Sweater shown measures 35½" (90 cm).

MATERIALS

yarn
Worsted weight (#4 Medium).

shown here: The Fibre Company Terra (40% baby alpaca, 40% merino wool, 20% silk; 98 yd [91 m]/50 g): yarrow (light blue; MC), 8 (9, 10, 11, 12, 13) skeins; logwood purple (CC1), hollyhock (pink; CC2), fustic (orange; CC3), anemone (pale green; CC4), 1 skein each.

needles
body: size U.S. 8 (5 mm): 16" (40 cm) and 24" or 36" (60 or 80 cm) circular (cir) and set of 4 or 5 double-pointed (dpn).

ribbing: size U.S. 6 (4 mm): 16" (40 cm) and 24" or 36" (60 or 80 cm) cir and set of 4 or 5 dpn.

Adjust needle size if necessary to obtain the correct gauge.

notions
Markers (m); waste yarn or spare needles for holders; tapestry needle.

gauge
18 stitches and 27 rounds = 4" (10 cm) in stockinette stitch on larger needle, worked in rounds; 19 stitches and 25 rounds = 4" (10 cm) in yoke pattern on larger needle, worked in rounds.

Stitch Guide

Broken Rib (even number of sts)

RND 1: *K1, p1; rep from *.

RND 2: Knit.

Rep Rnds 1 and 2 for patt.

Short-Rows

To update the look and fit of this sweater, short-rows are used to raise the back neck and shoulders. This creates a neckline that more closely resembles a crewneck, gives a more comfortable fit, and, when done correctly, is practically invisible. Short-row shaping may not seem clear as you read through the directions, but makes perfect sense when worked with the stitches on the needles.

When knitting short-rows, you'll work a section of the stitches back and forth in rows and wrap the working yarn around a stitch each time you change rows. This is commonly written as "wrap next st, turn," "wrap and turn," or "w&t." Here's how it works:

Right-Side (Knit) Rows

STEP 1: With the right (knit) side facing, knit to the turning point indicated in the written instructions.

STEP 2: Slip the next stitch purlwise (Figure 1).

STEP 3: Bring the working yarn to the front as if to purl the next stitch, then slip the same stitch back onto the left-hand needle (Figure 2) in preparation to knit the next stitch.

STEP 4: Turn the work around so that the wrong (purl) side is facing you, then bring the yarn into position for the next stitch—1 stitch has been wrapped, and the yarn is in position to purl the next stitch.

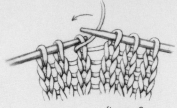

figure 2

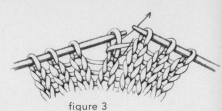

figure 3

To hide the wrap on a subsequent row, work to the wrapped stitch, insert the right needle tip under the wrap (Figure 3), then into the stitch on the needle, and work the stitch and its wrap together as a single stitch.

Wrong-Side (Purl) Rows

STEP 1: With the wrong (purl) side facing, purl to the turning point indicated in the written instructions.

STEP 2: Slip the next stitch purlwise, then bring the yarn to back of the work (Figure 4).

STEP 3: Return the slipped stitch to the left-hand needle, then bring the working yarn to the front (Figure 5).

STEP 4: Turn the work around so that the right (knit) side is facing you—1 stitch has been wrapped, and the yarn is in position to knit the next stitch.

To hide the wrap on a subsequent row, work to the wrapped stitch, use the tip of the right-hand needle to pick up the wrap from the back, place it on the left-hand needle (Figure 6), then work it together with the wrapped stitch.

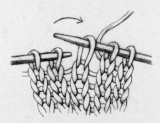

figure 1

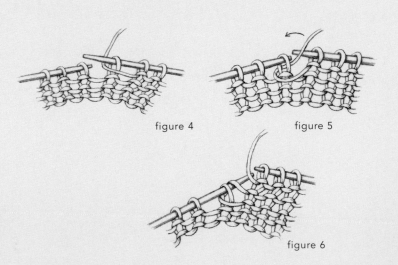

figure 4

figure 5

figure 6

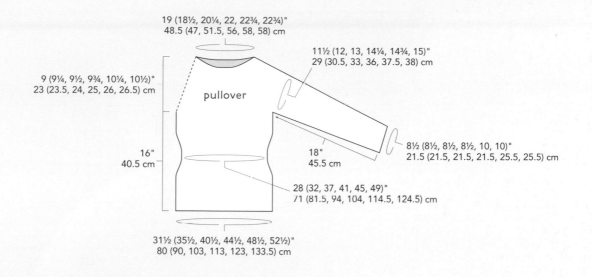

19 (18½, 20¼, 22, 22¾, 22¾)"
48.5 (47, 51.5, 56, 58, 58) cm

11½ (12, 13, 14¼, 14¾, 15)"
29 (30.5, 33, 36, 37.5, 38) cm

9 (9¼, 9½, 9¾, 10¼, 10½)"
23 (23.5, 24, 25, 26, 26.5) cm

pullover

16"
40.5 cm

8½ (8½, 8½, 8½, 10, 10)"
21.5 (21.5, 21.5, 21.5, 25.5, 25.5) cm

18"
45.5 cm

28 (32, 37, 41, 45, 49)"
71 (81.5, 94, 104, 114.5, 124.5) cm

31½ (35½, 40½, 44½, 48½, 52½)"
80 (90, 103, 113, 123, 133.5) cm

Sleeves

With MC and smaller dpn, CO 38 (38, 40, 40, 46, 46) sts.
Place marker (pm) and join for working in rnds, being careful
not to twist sts. Rep Rnds 1 and 2 of broken rib (see Stitch
Guide) 7 times, then rep Rnd 1 once more. Change to larger
dpn and work next rnd for your size as foll.

Sizes 31½ (35½, 48½, 52½) "
(80 [90, 123, 133.5] cm) only

K1, M1L (see page 78), knit to last st, M1R (see page 78),
k1—2 sts inc'd.

Sizes 40½ (44½)" (103 [113] cm) only

Knit.

All sizes

There are 40 (40, 40, 40, 48, 48) sts. Work Rnds 1–19 of
Sleeve chart (see page 73). Cont in MC only, work 3 rnds
even.

INC RND: K1, M1L, knit to last st, M1R, k1—2 sts inc'd.

Knit 6 rnds even. Rep the last 7 rnds 5 (6, 8, 11, 8, 9) more
times—52 (54, 58, 64, 66, 68) sts. Work even in St st until
piece measures 18" (45.5 cm) from CO or desired length to
underarm and *at the same time* work the last 2 rnds as foll:

Sleeve

19 17 15 13 11 9 7 5 3 1

Upper Yoke

9 7 5 3 1

Middle Yoke

15 13 11 9 7 5 3 1

Lower Yoke

9 7 5 3 1

× MC
◣ CC1
▬ CC2
+ CC3
| CC4
☐ pattern repeat

RND 1: Knit to last 4 sts, BO 4 sts—48 (50, 54, 60, 62, 64) sts rem.

RND 2: BO 4 sts, knit to end—44 (46, 50, 56, 58, 60) sts rem.

Place sts on waste yarn or spare needle.

Body

With MC and smaller, longer cir needle, CO 142 (160, 182, 200, 218, 236) sts. Pm and join for working in rnds, being careful not to twist sts. Rep Rnds 1 and 2 of broken rib until piece measures 3" (7.5 cm) from CO, ending with Rnd 2 of patt. Change to larger, longer cir needle and work even in St st for 2½" (6.5 cm).

NEXT RND: K71 (80, 91, 100, 109, 118), pm, knit to end.

DEC RND: K1, k2tog, knit to 3 sts before m, ssk, k1, slip marker (sl m), k1, k2tog, knit to last 3 sts, ssk, k1—4 sts dec'd.

Knit 6 rnds even. Rep the last 7 rnds 3 more times—126 (144, 166, 184, 202, 220) sts rem.

INC RND: K1, M1L, knit to 1 st before next m, M1R, k1, sl m, k1, M1L, knit to 1 st before next m, M1R, k1—4 sts inc'd.

Knit 6 rnds even. Rep the last 7 rnds 3 more times—142 (160, 182, 200, 218, 236) sts. Work even in St st until piece mea-

sures 16" (40.5 cm) from CO or desired length to underarm and *at the same time* work the last 2 rnds as foll:

RND 1: Knit to last 4 sts, BO 4 sts.

RND 2: BO 4 sts, knit to 4 sts before m, BO 8 sts, removing m as you come to it, knit to end—126 (144, 166, 184, 202, 220) sts rem; 63 (72, 83, 92, 101, 110) sts each for front and back.

Do not cut yarn.

Join for Yoke

Pm, k44 (46, 50, 56, 58, 60) held sleeve sts, pm, k63 (72, 83, 92, 101, 110) front sts, pm, k44 (46, 50, 56, 58, 60) held sleeve sts, pm, k63 (72, 83, 92, 101, 110) back sts—214 (236, 266, 296, 318, 340) sts total.

DEC RND: *K1, k2tog, knit to 3 sts before m, ssk, k1, sl m; rep from * 3 more times—8 sts dec'd.

Knit 1 rnd even. Rep the last 2 rnds 1 (1, 2, 3, 3, 3) more time(s)—198 (220, 242, 264, 286, 308) sts rem.

SHORT-ROW SET-UP ROW: K17, pm, knit to next m, remove m, knit to next m, remove m, knit to 17 sts before next m, pm, knit to next m, remove m, knit to end of rnd.

Work short-rows (see page 70) as foll:

SHORT-ROW 1: Knit to 1 st before first m, wrap next st, turn work.

SHORT-ROW 2: (WS) Purl to end-of-rnd m, sl m, purl to 1 st before next m, wrap next st, turn work.

SHORT-ROW 3: Knit to 8 sts before last wrapped st (slipping m when you come to it), wrap next st, turn work.

SHORT-ROW 4: Purl to 8 sts before last wrapped st (slipping m when you come to it), wrap next st, turn work.

Rep Short-Rows 3 and 4 four (five, five, five, five, five) more times.

NEXT RND: With RS facing, knit to end of rnd, working wraps tog with wrapped sts as you go.

Knit 1 rnd, working rem wraps tog with wrapped sts.

Sizes 48½ (52½)" (123 [133.5] cm) only
Work even in St st for ½ (¾)" (1.3 [2] cm).

All sizes
DEC RND: *K1, k2tog, k17, ssk; rep from *—180 (200, 220, 240, 260, 280) sts rem.

Fair Isle Yoke

Work Rnds 1–9 of Lower Yoke chart.

DEC RND 1: With CC4, work as specified for your size:

Size 31½" (80 cm) only: *K7, k2tog; rep from *—160 sts rem.

Size 35½" (90 cm) only: *K6, k2tog, k6, k2tog, k7, k2tog; rep from *—176 sts rem.

Size 40½" (103 cm) only: K2tog, k4, *k2tog, k6; rep from * to last 6 sts, k2tog, k4—192 sts rem.

Size 44½" (113 cm) only: *K5, k2tog, k6, k2tog; rep from *—208 sts rem.

Size 48½" (123 cm) only: *[K5, k2tog] 3 times, k6, k2tog; rep from * to last 28 sts, [k5, k2tog] 4 times—224 sts rem.

Size 52½" (133.5 cm) only: *K5, k2tog; rep from *—240 sts rem.

Work Rnds 1–16 of Middle Yoke chart.

DEC RND 2: With CC4, work as specified for your size:

Sizes 31½ (35½, 40½, 44½)" (80 [90, 103, 113] cm) only: *K2, k2tog; rep from *—120 (132, 144, 156) sts rem.

Size 48½" (123 cm) only: *K1, k2tog, k2, k2tog; rep from *—160 sts rem.

Size 52½" (133.5 cm) only: *K1, k2tog; rep from * —160 sts rem.

Work Rnds 1–9 of Upper Yoke chart.

DEC RND 3: With MC, work as specified for your size:

Size 31½" (80 cm) only: *K2, k2tog; rep from *—90 sts rem.

Sizes 35½ (40½, 44½, 48½, 52½)" (90 [103, 113, 123, 133.5] cm) only: *K1, k2tog; rep from * to last 0 (0, 0, 4, 4) sts, knit to end—88 (96, 104, 108, 108) sts rem.

Neckband
Change to smaller, shorter cir needle. Rep Rnds 1 and 2 of broken rib patt 2 times, then work Rnd 1 once more. BO all sts.

Finishing
Weave in loose ends. Block to measurements.

Abigail HAND WARMERS

DESIGNED BY COURTNEY KELLEY

These hand warmers are a nice update on traditional Norwegian Selbu mittens and gloves. The name *Selbu* is
taken from the mountainous region around Lake Selbu where
the design style was popularized for the tourist trade in the
mid-1800s. Historically, Selbu mittens were knitted in an intricate symmetrical pattern of black and white, featuring the
star-point and rose motifs popular in decorative folk arts of
the region. The pattern in this pair, inspired by a Victorian-
era wallpaper print, adds a bit of feminine flair and vintage
appeal without losing the traditional look or feel. Worked in
mint green and plum, they bring a touch of spring warmth to a
cold winter day. An extralong cuff keeps wrists warm with old-
fashioned elegance.

MATERIALS

yarn
Fingering weight (#1 Super Fine).

shown here: The Fibre Company
Canopy Fingering (50% baby alpaca,
30% merino wool, 20% bamboo;
200 yd [183 m]/50 g): fern (MC) and
plum (CC), 1 skein each.

needles
cuff: size U.S. 1 (2.25 mm): set of 4 or
5 double-pointed (dpn).

hand: size U.S. 2 (2.75 mm): set of 4 or
5 dpn.

*Adjust needle size if necessary to
obtain the correct gauge*

notions
Markers (m); waste yarn or stitch
holder; tapestry needle.

gauge
36 stitches and 40 rounds = 4" (10 cm)
in hand pattern on larger needles,
worked in rounds.

finished size
About 7¾" (19.5 cm) hand circumference and 10¼" (26 cm) in length.
To fit a women's small to medium hand.

Mirrored Increases

When working increases for a thumb gusset (or any set of paired increases) it's wise to mirror the increases so they appear symmetrical. A make-one (M1) increase is made by picking up the running thread and knitting into it. The running thread is the yarn just below your needles that connects one stitch to another. For instance, if you are in the middle of knitted row or round, take a close look at the first stitch on each needle. The first stitch on the left-hand needle goes up and over the needle; follow that thread with your eyes—it goes across the gap to the stitch below the first stitch on the right-hand needle. Where it bridges the gap is what we call the "running thread." When making the gusset increases, the first increase should slant to the left—a M1L increase. The second gusset increase should slant to the right—a M1R increase.

Make-One Left (M1L)

Note: Use the M1L method if no direction is specified.

STEP 1. Place the running thread onto the left-hand needle with the right leg of the thread in front (Figure 1); note that it sits the "right way" on the needle.

STEP 2. Knit into the back of the stitch (Figure 2).

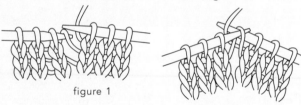

figure 1   figure 2

Make-One Right (M1R)

STEP 1. Place the running thread onto the left-hand needle with the left leg of the thread in front (Figure 3); note that it sits the "wrong way" on the needle.

STEP 2. Knit into the front of this stitch (Figure 4).

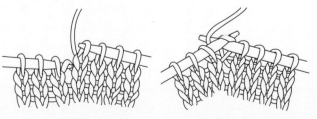

figure 3   figure 4

Cuff

With CC and smaller needles, CO 68 sts. Divide sts as evenly as possible on 3 or 4 needles, place marker (pm), and join for working in rnds, being careful not to twist sts. Beg with a purl rnd, work 10 rnds in garter st (alternate purl 1 rnd, knit 1 rnd). Change to larger needles and St st (knit every rnd). With CC, knit 1 rnd. Work Rnds 1–43 of Cuff chart. With CC, knit 1 rnd—piece measures about 4¾" (12 cm) from CO.

Cuff

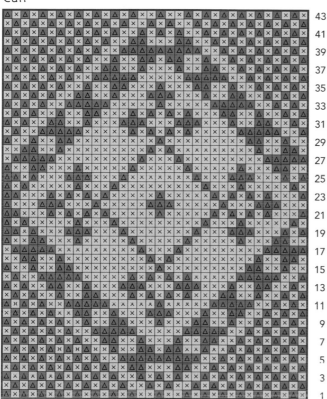

43
41
39
37
35
33
31
29
27
25
23
21
19
17
15
13
11
9
7
5
3
1

×	MC
△	CC
MR	M1R with MC
MR	M1R with CC
ML	M1L with MC
ML	M1L with CC
☐	pattern repeat

Hand

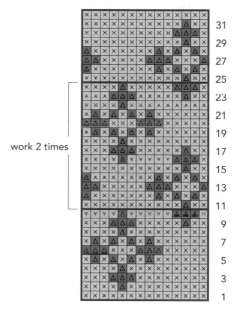

31
29
27
25
23
21
19
17
15
13
11
9
7
5
3
1

work 2 times

Thumb

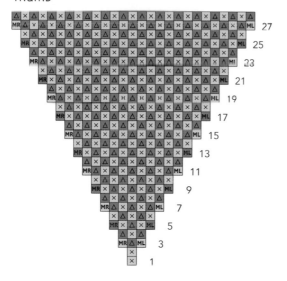

27
25
23
21
19
17
15
13
11
9
7
5
3
1

Hand

NEXT RND: *K1 with MC, k1 with CC; rep from * to end of rnd.

INC RND: With CC, knit and *at the same time* inc 2 sts evenly spaced—70 sts.

Work Rnds 1–10 of Hand chart.

Thumb Gusset

SET-UP RND: (Rnd 11 of chart) M1 (see page 78) with MC, pm, work to end of rnd—1 gusset st between markers.

Cont working Hand chart as established and *at the same time* work Rnds 1–28 of Thumb chart over gusset st, inc as indicated on chart—27 gusset sts. Place 27 gusset sts on waste yarn or holder. Work through Rnd 32 of Hand chart. With MC, knit 1 rnd. Change to smaller needles and CC. Beg with a knit rnd, work 6 rnds in garter st. Loosely BO all sts.

Thumb

Arrange 27 held gusset sts on 3 or 4 larger needles. With CC, k27 gusset sts, then pick up and knit 1 st at gap between hand and thumb—28 sts total. Beg with a purl rnd, work 3 rnds in garter st. Loosely BO all sts.

Finishing

Weave in loose ends. Block to measurements.

Yangtze CARDIGAN

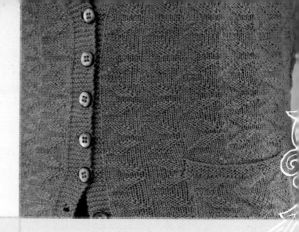

DESIGNED BY COURTNEY KELLEY

This cardigan represents the classic 1950s cardigan I have always dreamed of, updated slightly for a more comfortable fit. A feminine, flattering, and tailored silhouette paired with an elegant textured pattern results in a sweater that is worth every stitch. Suited equally to a tank top and slouchy jeans or a wool tweed skirt and silk blouse, this basic cardigan is poised to be an heirloom classic. The blend of alpaca, merino, and bamboo creates a soft fabric with gentle drape that has a great balance of warmth and sheen and produces a garment with a sophisticated look you can be proud to say you made yourself.

MATERIALS

yarn
Fingering weight (#1 Super Fine).

shown here: The Fibre Company Canopy Fingering (50% baby alpaca, 30% merino wool, 20% bamboo; 200 yd [183 m]/50 g): river dolphin, 8 (9, 10, 11, 12, 13, 15) balls.

needles
body and sleeves: size U.S. 2 (2.75 mm): straight or 24" (60 cm) circular (cir).

cuffs and hem: size U.S. 1 (2.25 mm): straight or 24" (60 cm) cir.

Adjust needle size if necessary to obtain the correct gauge.

notions
Marker (m); stitch holders; tapestry needle; eight (eight, six, six, six, five, five) ½" (1.3 cm) buttons.

gauge
31 stitches and 48 rows = 4" (10 cm) in pattern on larger needles.

finished size
About 31 (34, 36½, 39, 41½, 44, 46½)" (78.5 [86.5, 92.5, 99, 105.5, 112, 118] cm) bust circumference, buttoned. Sweater shown measures 31" (78.5 cm).

Note

> The row gauge is very important, as it is related to the spacing of the shaping. All increases and decreases except for armhole, back neck, and sleeve cap shaping are worked on Rows 2 and 10 of the stitch pattern.

Grafting for Garter Stitch

Garter stitch, typically worked by knitting every stitch of every row, forms a reversible fabric with alternating rows of smooth knit stitches and purl bumps (even though no purling is required, purl bumps form on the wrong side of knit stitches). The key to grafting garter stitch is to keep the sequence of purl bumps or ridges and knit valleys intact. Grafting, worked with yarn threaded on a tapestry needle, adds a row of "knitting" to the two pieces to be joined. It is worked between two sets of the same number of live stitches. Each set is held on a separate needle.

For this design, the 8-stitch front bands extend into a narrow collar that is grafted at the back neck. There are 8 live right neck stitches and 8 live left neck stitches. Place each group of 8 stitches onto a separate double-pointed needle and lay the work on a flat surface with the right side facing up. Determine whether the last row worked on each group appears as a knit valley or purl ridge on the right side. Make sure that there is a knit valley at the base of the left neck stitches and a purl ridge at the base of the right neck stitches.

Hold the two pieces so that the needle with the purl ridge (right neck stitches) is behind the needle with the knit valley (left neck stitches). Thread a 10" (25.5 cm) length of yarn (use the yarn attached to the neck stitches to avoid joining new yarn) on a tapestry needle. You will use the tapestry needle to form purl ridges on the front needle (the left neck stitches) and knit valleys on the back needle (the right neck stitches).

Most grafting instructions say to insert the tapestry needle through the live stitches "as if to knit" or "as if to purl." I prefer to think of the movements as "down" or "up." To insert the tapestry needle "down," insert it downward into the stitch, moving it away from your body. To insert the tapestry needle "up," insert it upward through the stitch, moving it from the back of the work toward your body.

Note: In the illustrations, the "back" needle is shown as the upper needle; the "front" needle is shown as the lower needle.

STEP 1: To set up, insert the tapestry needle down (from front to back) through the first stitch on the lower needle, then up (wrong side to right side) through the first stitch on the upper needle (Figure 1).

STEP 2: Insert the tapestry needle up through the first stitch on the lower needle (the same stitch entered in Step 1), slip this stitch off the needle, then insert the tapestry needle down through the next stitch on the lower needle (Figure 2).

STEP 3: Insert the tapestry needle down through the first stitch on the upper needle (the same stitch entered in Step 1), slip this stitch off the needle, then insert the tapestry needle up through the next stitch on the upper needle (Figure 3).

To continue, repeat this simple mantra:

STEP 1: Up in front; slip off.

STEP 2: Down in front; leave on.

STEP 3: Down in back; slip off.

STEP 4: Up in back; leave on.

Repeat these four steps until all stitches have been grafted, ending by inserting the tapestry needle up through the last stitch on the lower needle, then down through the last stitch on the upper needle (Figure 4). Tighten the grafted sts to match the knitted tension. Weave the tail into the wrong side of the work.

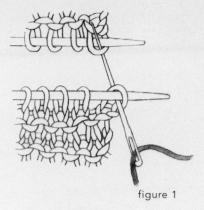

figure 1

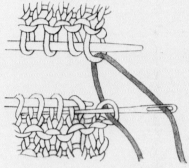

figure 2

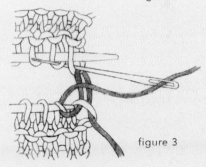

figure 3

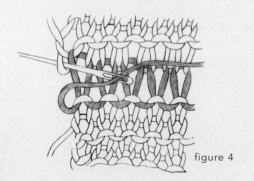

figure 4

Back

With smaller needles, CO 121 (131, 141, 151, 161, 171, 181) sts. Work in garter st (knit every row) until piece measures 1" (2.5 cm) from CO, ending with a RS row. Change to larger needles and work Rows 1–16 of Parallelogram chart (see page 87) 1 (1, 2, 2, 3, 3, 4) time(s)—piece measures about 2¼ (2¼, 3¾, 3¾, 5, 5, 6¼)" (5.5 [5.5, 9.5, 9.5, 12.5, 12.5, 16] cm) from CO. Cont in patt, [dec 1 st each end of needle on Row 2 and Row 10 of patt] 3 times as foll: K1, ssk, knit to last 3 sts, k2tog, k1—2 sts dec'd each dec row; 109 (119, 129, 139, 149, 159, 169) sts rem after all decs have been worked. Work Rows 11–16, then work Rows 1–9 once more. Cont in patt, [inc 1 st each end of needle on Row 10 and Row 2 of patt] 3 times as foll: K1, k1f&b (see Glossary), knit to last 2 sts, k1f&b, k1—2 sts inc'd each inc row; 121 (131, 141, 151, 161, 171, 181) sts after all incs have been worked. Cont even in patt until piece measures about 15 (16, 16, 16, 17, 17, 18)" (38 [40.5, 40.5, 40.5, 43, 43, 45.5] cm) from CO, ending with Row 15 of patt.

Shape Armholes

BO 7 (8, 8, 9, 9, 12, 12) sts at beg of next 2 rows—107 (115, 125, 133, 143, 147, 157) sts rem.

DEC ROW: (RS) K1, ssk, work to last 3 sts, k2tog, k1—2 sts dec'd.

Cont in patt, dec 1 st each end of needle in this manner every RS row 5 (5, 5, 6, 9, 9, 9) more times—95 (103, 113, 119, 123, 127, 137) sts rem. Cont even in patt until armholes measure 5½ (6, 6½, 7, 7½, 8, 8½)" (14 [15, 16.5, 18, 19, 20.5, 21.5] cm), ending with a WS row.

Shape Neck

Cont in patt, work 34 (34, 34, 36, 38, 40, 44) sts, join second ball of yarn and BO next 27 (35, 45, 47, 47, 47, 49) sts, work to end—34 (34, 34, 36, 38, 40, 44) sts rem each side. Working each side separately, dec 1 st at each neck edge every RS row 6 times—28 (28, 28, 30, 32, 34, 38) sts rem each side.

Shape Shoulders

At each armhole edge, BO 10 (10, 10, 10, 12, 12, 14) sts once, then BO 10 (10, 10, 10, 10, 12, 12) sts once, then BO rem 8 (8, 8, 10, 10, 10, 12) sts.

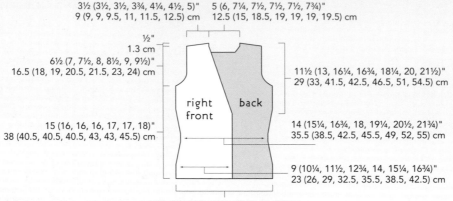

3½ (3½, 3½, 3¾, 4¼, 4½, 5)"
9 (9, 9, 9.5, 11, 11.5, 12.5) cm

5 (6, 7¼, 7½, 7½, 7½, 7¾)"
12.5 (15, 18.5, 19, 19, 19, 19.5) cm

½"
1.3 cm

6½ (7, 7½, 8, 8½, 9, 9½)"
16.5 (18, 19, 20.5, 21.5, 23, 24) cm

11½ (13, 16¼, 16¾, 18¼, 20, 21½)"
29 (33, 41.5, 42.5, 46.5, 51, 54.5) cm

right front

back

15 (16, 16, 16, 17, 17, 18)"
38 (40.5, 40.5, 40.5, 43, 43, 45.5) cm

14 (15¼, 16¾, 18, 19¼, 20½, 21¾)"
35.5 (38.5, 42.5, 45.5, 49, 52, 55) cm

9 (10¼, 11½, 12¾, 14, 15¼, 16¾)"
23 (26, 29, 32.5, 35.5, 38.5, 42.5) cm

15½ (17, 18¼, 19½, 20¾, 22, 23¼)"
39.5 (43, 46.5, 49.5, 52.5, 56, 59) cm

1¼ (1, 2½, 2¾, 3, 1¾, 1½)"
3.2 (2.5, 6.5, 7, 7.5, 4.5, 3.8) cm

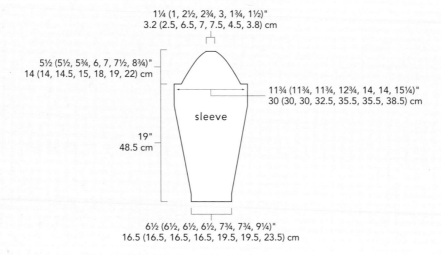

5½ (5½, 5¾, 6, 7, 7½, 8¾)"
14 (14, 14.5, 15, 18, 19, 22) cm

11¾ (11¾, 11¾, 12¾, 14, 14, 15¼)"
30 (30, 30, 32.5, 35.5, 35.5, 38.5) cm

sleeve

19"
48.5 cm

6½ (6½, 6½, 6½, 7¾, 7¾, 9¼)"
16.5 (16.5, 16.5, 16.5, 19.5, 19.5, 23.5) cm

Pocket Lining (make 2)

With larger needles, CO 30 sts. Work in St st (knit RS rows; purl WS rows) until piece measures 4" (10 cm) from CO. Place sts on holder.

Left Front

With smaller needles, CO 69 (79, 89, 99, 109, 119, 129) sts. Work in garter st until piece measures 1" (2.5 cm) from CO, ending with a RS row. Change to larger needles.

Shape Waist

Note: Pocket lining is inserted while waist shaping is worked or before it is begun, and neck shaping beg while waist shaping is worked; read the foll sections all the way through before proceeding.

NEXT ROW: (WS) Work 8 sts in garter st, place marker (pm), work Row 1 of Parallelogram chart to end.

Cont in patt until Rows 1–16 of chart have been worked 1 (1, 2, 2, 3, 3, 4) time(s), then shape waist as foll: Cont in patt, [dec 1 st at side edge on Row 2 and Row 10 of patt] 3 times

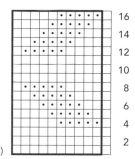

as foll: K1, ssk, work in patt to end—1 st dec'd each dec row; 6 sts dec'd total. Work Rows 11–16, then work Rows 1–9 once more. Cont in patt, [inc 1 st at side edge on Row 10 and Row 2 of patt] 3 times as foll: K1, k1f&b, work in patt to end—1 st inc'd each inc row; 6 sts inc'd total.

Insert Pocket

At the same time when the 16-row rep has been worked 3 times (48 patt rows), work Row 1 once more, then insert pocket lining as foll: (Row 2 of patt) Working waist shaping as established, work to last 57 sts, place next 30 sts on a holder, k30 held pocket lining sts, work in patt to end.

Also at the same time cont in patt until the 16-row rep has been worked 7 (7, 5, 5, 5, 4, 4) times total, work Row 1 once more, then beg neck shaping.

Shape Neck

Note: Armhole shaping beg before neck shaping ends; read the foll sections all the way through before proceeding.

Dec for neck on Row 2 and Row 10 of patt for your size as foll.

Size 31" (78.5 cm) only

ON ROWS 2 AND 10: Work in patt to 3 sts before m, k2tog, knit to end—1 st dec'd each row.

Rep these 2 rows 4 more times—10 sts dec'd.

NEXT ROW 2: Work in patt to 3 sts before m, k2tog, knit to end—1 st dec'd.

NEXT ROW 10: Work in patt to 4 sts before m, k3tog, knit to end—2 sts dec'd.

Rep these 2 rows 2 more times, then work Row 2 once more—10 sts dec'd; 20 neck sts dec'd total.

Size 34" (86.5 cm) only

ON ROW 2: Work in patt to 3 sts before m, k2tog, knit to end—1 st dec'd.

ON ROW 10: Work in patt to 4 sts before m, k3tog, knit to end—2 sts dec'd.

Rep these 2 rows 8 more times—27 sts dec'd.

NEXT ROW 2: Work in patt to 4 sts before m, k3tog, knit to end—2 sts dec'd; 29 neck sts dec'd total.

Size 36½" (92.5 cm) only

ON ROW 2: Work in patt to 3 sts before m, k2tog, knit to end—1 st dec'd.

ON ROW 10: Work in patt to 4 sts before m, k3tog, knit to end—2 sts dec'd.

Rep these 2 rows 4 more times—15 sts dec'd.

NEXT ROWS 2 AND 10: Work in patt to 4 sts before m, k3tog, knit to end—2 sts dec'd each row.

Rep these 2 rows 5 more times—24 sts dec'd; 39 neck sts dec'd total.

Size 39" (99 cm) only

ON ROW 2: Work in patt to 3 sts before m, k2tog, knit to end—1 st dec'd.

ON ROW 10: Work in patt to 4 sts before m, k3tog, knit to end—2 sts dec'd.

Rep these 2 rows 2 more times—9 sts dec'd.

NEXT ROWS 2 AND 10: Work in patt to 4 sts before m, k3tog, knit to end—2 sts dec'd each row.

Rep these 2 rows 8 more times—36 sts dec'd; 45 neck sts dec'd total.

Size 41½" (105.5 cm) only

ON ROWS 2 AND 10: Work in patt to 3 sts before m, k2tog, knit to end—1 st dec'd each row; 2 sts dec'd total.

NEXT ROWS 2 AND 10: Work in patt to 4 sts before m, k3tog, knit to end—2 sts dec'd each row.

Rep these 2 rows 11 more times—48 sts dec'd; 50 neck sts dec'd total.

Sizes 44 (46½)" (112 [118] cm) only

ON ROW 2: Work in patt to 3 sts before m, k2tog, knit to end—1 st dec'd.

ON ROW 10: Work in patt to 4 sts before m, k3tog, knit to end—2 sts dec'd; 3 sts dec'd total.

NEXT ROWS 2 AND 10: Work in patt to 4 sts before m, k3tog, knit to end—2 sts dec'd each row.

Rep these 2 rows 12 (13) more times, then work Row 2 zero (one) more time—52 (58) sts dec'd; 55 (61) neck sts dec'd total.

All sizes

At the same time work until piece measures same as back to armhole, ending with Row 15 of patt.

Shape Armhole

Cont working neck shaping, at armhole edge (beg of RS rows), BO 7 (8, 8, 9, 9, 12, 12) sts. Work 1 (WS) row even.

DEC ROW: (RS) K1, ssk, work to end of row—1 armhole st dec'd.

Dec 1 st at armhole edge every RS row in this manner 5 (5, 5, 6, 9, 9, 9) more times. Work until armhole measures 6½ (7, 7½, 8, 8½, 9, 9½)" (16.5 [18, 19, 20.5, 21.5, 23, 24] cm), end-

ing with a WS row—36 (36, 36, 38, 40, 42, 46) sts rem when all armhole and neck shaping is complete.

Shape Shoulder

Cont in patt, at armhole edge (beg of RS rows), BO 10 (10, 10, 10, 12, 12, 14) sts once, then BO 10 (10, 10, 10, 10, 12, 12) sts once, then BO 8 (8, 8, 10, 10, 10, 12) sts once—8 sts rem for buttonband. Place sts on holder.

Right Front

With smaller needles, CO 69 (79, 89, 99, 109, 119, 129) sts. Work in garter st until piece measures 1" (2.5 cm) from CO, ending with a RS row. Change to larger needles.

Shape Waist

Note: Buttonholes are worked until neck shaping beg, pocket lining is inserted while waist shaping is worked or before it is begun, and neck shaping beg while waist shaping is worked; read the foll sections all the way through before proceeding.

NEXT ROW: (WS; buttonhole row) Work Row 1 of Parallelogram chart to last 8 sts, pm, k3, BO 3 sts, knit to end.

On the next row, use the cable method (see Glossary) to CO 3 sts over gap formed on previous row. Rep buttonhole on every Row 1 of chart to beg of neck shaping. *At the same time* work in patt until Rows 1–16 of chart have been worked 1 (1, 2, 2, 3, 3, 4) time(s), then shape waist as foll: Cont in patt, [dec 1 st at side edge on Row 2 and Row 10 of patt] 3 times as foll: Work in patt to last 3 sts, k2tog, k1—1 st dec'd each dec row; 6 sts dec'd total. Work Rows 11–16, then work Rows 1–9 once more. Cont in patt, [inc 1 st at side edge on Row 10 and Row 2 of patt] 3 times as foll: Work in patt to last 2 sts, k1f&b, k1—1 st inc'd each inc row; 6 sts inc'd total.

Insert Pocket

Also at the same time when the 16-row rep has been worked 3 times (48 patt rows), work Row 1 once more, then insert pocket lining as foll: (Row 2 of patt) Work 27 sts in patt, place next 30 sts on a holder, k30 held pocket lining sts, work in patt to end of row while working waist shaping as established.

Also at the same time cont in patt until the 16-row rep has been worked 7 (7, 5, 5, 5, 4, 4) times total, work Row 1 once more, then beg neck shaping.

Shape Neck

Note: Armhole shaping beg before neck shaping ends; read the foll sections all the way through before proceeding.

Dec for neck on Row 2 and Row 10 of patt for your size as foll.

Size 31" (78.5 cm) only

ON ROWS 2 AND 10: Knit to m, k1, ssk, work in patt to end—1 st dec'd each row.

Rep these 2 rows 4 more times—10 sts dec'd.

NEXT ROW 2: Knit to m, k1, ssk, work in patt to end—1 st dec'd.

NEXT ROW 10: Knit to m, k1, sssk (see Glossary), work in patt to end—2 sts dec'd.

Rep these 2 rows 2 more times, then work Row 2 once more—10 sts dec'd; 20 neck sts dec'd total.

Size 34" (86.5 cm) only

ON ROW 2: Knit to m, k1, ssk, work in patt to end—1 st dec'd.

ON ROW 10: Knit to m, k1, sssk (see Glossary), work in patt to end—2 sts dec'd.

Rep these 2 rows 8 more times—27 sts dec'd.

NEXT ROW 2: Knit to m, k1, sssk, work in patt to end—2 sts dec'd; 29 neck sts dec'd total.

Size 36½" (92.5 cm) only

ON ROW 2: Knit to m, k1, ssk, work in patt to end—1 st dec'd.

ON ROW 10: Knit to m, k1, sssk (see Glossary), work in patt to end—2 sts dec'd.

Rep these 2 rows 4 more times—15 sts dec'd.

NEXT ROWS 2 AND 10: Knit to m, k1, sssk, work in patt to end—2 sts dec'd each row.

Rep these 2 rows 5 more times—24 sts dec'd; 39 neck sts dec'd total.

Size 39" (99 cm) only

ON ROW 2: Knit to m, k1, ssk, work in patt to end—1 st dec'd.

ON ROW 10: Knit to m, k1, sssk (see Glossary), work in patt to end—2 sts dec'd.

Rep these 2 rows 2 more times—9 sts dec'd.

NEXT ROWS 2 AND 10: Knit to m, k1, sssk, work in patt to end—2 sts dec'd each row.

Rep these 2 rows 8 more times—36 sts dec'd; 45 neck sts dec'd total.

Size 41½" (105.5 cm) only

ON ROWS 2 AND 10: Knit to m, k1, ssk, work in patt to end—1 st dec'd each row; 2 sts dec'd total.

NEXT ROWS 2 AND 10: Knit to m, k1, sssk (see Glossary), work in patt to end—2 sts dec'd each row.

Rep these 2 rows 11 more times—48 sts dec'd; 50 neck sts dec'd total.

Sizes 44 (46½)" (112 [118] cm) only

ON ROW 2: Knit to m, k1, ssk, work in patt to end—1 st dec'd.

ON ROW 10: Knit to m, k1, sssk (see Glossary), work in patt to end—2 sts dec'd; 3 sts dec'd total.

NEXT ROWS 2 AND 10: Knit to m, k1, sssk, work in patt to end—2 sts dec'd each row.

Rep these 2 rows 12 (13) more times, then work Row 2 zero (one) more time—52 (58) sts dec'd; 55 (61) neck sts dec'd total.

All sizes

At the same time work until piece measures same as back to armhole, ending with row 16 of patt.

Shape Armhole

Cont working neck shaping, at armhole edge (beg of WS row), BO 7 (8, 8, 9, 9, 12, 12) sts.

DEC ROW: (RS) Work to last 3 sts, k2tog, k1—1 armhole st dec'd.

Dec 1 st at armhole edge every RS row in this manner 5 (5, 5, 6, 9, 9, 9) more times. Work until armhole measures 6½ (7, 7½,

8, 8½, 9, 9½)" (16.5 [18, 19, 20.5, 21.5, 23, 24] cm), ending with a RS row—36 (36, 36, 38, 40, 42, 46) sts rem when all armhole and neck shaping is complete.

Shape Shoulder

Cont in patt, at armhole edge (beg of WS rows), BO 10 (10, 10, 10, 12, 12, 14) sts once, then BO 10 (10, 10, 10, 10, 12, 12) sts once, then BO 8 (8, 8, 10, 10, 10, 12) sts once—8 sts rem for buttonhole band. Place sts on holder.

Sleeves

With smaller needles, CO 51 (51, 51, 51, 61, 61, 71) sts. Work in garter st for 10 rows. Change to larger needles. Work Rows 1–9 of Parallelogram chart.

INC ROW: (Row 10 of chart) K1, M1 (see page 78), work to last st, M1, k1—2 sts inc'd.

Rep inc row on every Row 2 and Row 10 of chart until a total of 20 (20, 20, 24, 24, 24, 24) inc rows have been worked, working new sts into patt—91 (91, 91, 99, 109, 109, 119) sts. Cont even in patt until piece measures 19" (48.5 cm) from CO or desired length to underarm, ending with a WS row.

Shape Cap

BO 7 (8, 8, 9, 9, 12, 12) sts at beg of next 2 rows—77 (75, 75, 81, 91, 85, 95) sts rem.

DEC ROW: (RS) K1, ssk, work in patt to last 3 sts, k2tog, k1—2 sts dec'd.

Working the first 3 and last 3 sts in St st and the center sts in patt as established, rep dec row every RS row 7 (7, 7, 9, 9, 11, 13) more times—61 (59, 59, 61, 71, 61, 67) sts rem. Rep dec row every 4th row 6 (6, 8, 8, 10, 10, 12) times—49 (47, 43, 45, 51, 41, 43) sts rem. Rep dec row every RS row 6 (6, 8, 8, 10, 10, 12) times—37 (35, 27, 29, 31, 21, 19) sts rem.

Sizes 31 (34)" (78.5 [86.5] cm) only

NEXT ROW: (RS) K1, ssk, work in patt to last 3 sts, k2tog, k1—2 sts dec'd.

NEXT ROW: (WS) P1, p2tog, work in patt to last 3 sts, ssp (see Glossary), p1—2 sts dec'd.

Rep the last 2 rows 4 more times—17 (15) sts rem.

BO 2 sts at the beg of the next 4 rows—9 (7, 19, 21, 23, 13, 11) sts rem. BO all sts.

Finishing

Weave in loose ends. Block to measurements. With yarn threaded on a tapestry needle, sew fronts to back at shoulders. Sew sleeve caps into armholes. Sew sleeve and side seams.

Pocket Edging

With RS facing, place 30 held pocket sts onto smaller needles. Work 6 rows in garter st. With RS facing, BO all sts pwise. Sew sides of pocket edging to sweater front. Sew pocket lining to WS of sweater.

Neckband

Place 8 left front buttonband sts on smaller needle. With WS facing, *k7, sl 1 kwise with yarn in front (wyf), pick up and purl (see Glossary) 1 st along back neck, psso. Turn work, sl 1 with yarn in back (wyb), k7; rep from * to center of back neck, picking up 4 sts total along shaped edge and 8 (10, 13, 14, 14, 14, 15) sts evenly spaced across back neck BO. Place sts on holder.

Place 8 right front buttonhole band sts on smaller needle. With RS facing, *k7, sl 1 kwise wyb, pick up and knit 1 st along back neck, psso. Turn work, k8; rep from * to center of back neck, picking up 4 sts total along shaped edge and 8 (10, 13, 14, 14, 14, 15) sts evenly spaced across back neck BO.

With yarn threaded on a tapestry needle and using grafting for garter st (see page 84), graft 8 buttonband sts to 8 buttonhole band sts.

Baltic MITTENS + BERET

DESIGNED BY KATE GAGNON OSBORN

Color-stranded knitwear designs produced by the Swedish Bohus Knitting Workshop were famous in the late 1930s to the 1960s for their attention to detail, innovative design and color, and exacting standards of craftsmanship. Traditionally worked in a fine-weight blend of angora and merino that created a gorgeous halo, the color-stranded patterns were punctuated with purl stitches and sometimes a third—or fourth or fifth—color per row. While different from authentic Bohus knitting in fiber content and gauge, this mitten-and-beret set takes inspiration from that beautiful work by combining four tones of fingering-weight yarn in a geometric pattern accented by purl stitches and a third color every few rounds for optimal effect. The mittens have a stockinette stitch lining that provides an additional layer of warmth and softness.

finished size

mittens: About 8½" (21.5 cm) outer mitten circumference and 11" (28 cm) long. To fit 7½" (19 cm) palm circumference.

beret: About 16" (40.5 cm) unstretched brim circumference, 21" (53.5 cm) stretched brim circumference, 24¾" (63 cm) widest circumference, and 8½" (21.5 cm) long from cast-on to top of beret.

MATERIALS

yarn
Fingering weight (#1 Super Fine).

shown here: The Fibre Company Canopy Fingering (50% baby alpaca, 30% merino wool, 20% bamboo; 200 yd [183 m]/50 g). blue quandons (MC), 2 skeins; palm bud (lavender; CC1), fern (green; CC2), and orchid (white; CC3), 1 skein each.

needles
mitten hand: size U.S. 3 (3.25 mm): set of 4 or 5 double-pointed (dpn).

mitten cuff and lining: size U.S. 1 (2.25 mm): set of 4 or 5 dpn.

beret body: size U.S. 3 (3.25 mm): set of 4 or 5 dpn and 20" (50 cm) circular (cir).

beret ribbing: size U.S. 1 (2.25 mm): 16" (40 cm) cir.

Adjust needle size if necessary to obtain the correct gauge.

notions
Smooth waste yarn of comparable gauge; markers (m); stitch holders; tapestry needle.

gauge
31 stitches and 33 rounds = 4" (10 cm) in charted pattern on larger needles, worked in rounds.

Bohus Knitting Tips

Bohus knitting is deceptively simple—there are just a few things to keep in mind for optimum results.

> After purling a stitch, be sure to move the yarn to the back of the work before knitting the next stitch.

> When working with more than two colors per row, it is imperative to assign "placement" of the yarns as they are carried across the back of the work. Instead of just one yarn carried "over" and another carried "under," you will also have a yarn carried in the middle. Be sure to maintain constant placement of these yarns throughout the row.

> When choosing your own color combination, consider how yarns interact with one another in the colorwork pattern as well as how the purl stitch will affect the color it "pops up" from the row below.

> For the mittens, carry the unused yarns up the inside of the work—there is no need to cut and weave in additional ends because the lining will hide the inside of your work. Additionally, prior to starting the decreases on the mitten lining (after you've knitted an inch or so above the thumb opening), take the time to weave in all remaining ends (except for your working yarn, of course!). Once the top of hand and thumb are finished off, you will not have access to the inside (WS) of your work.

Hand

With MC, waste yarn, smaller dpn, and using a provisional method (see Glossary), CO 58 sts. Arrange sts as evenly as possible on 3 or 4 dpn, place marker (pm), and join for working in rnds, being careful not to twist sts. Work Rnds 1–9 of Mitten chart, inc as indicated on chart—66 sts. Change to larger dpn. Work Rnds 10–47 of chart.

Thumb Opening

Work next rnd (Rnd 48 of chart) as foll:

RIGHT MITTEN: Work in patt to right thumb sts, place 11 thumb sts on holder, use the backward-loop method (see Glossary) and MC to CO 11 sts over held sts, work in patt to end of rnd.

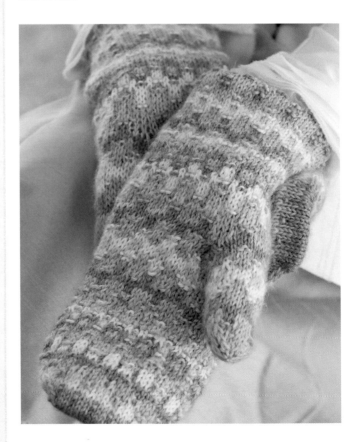

Mitten

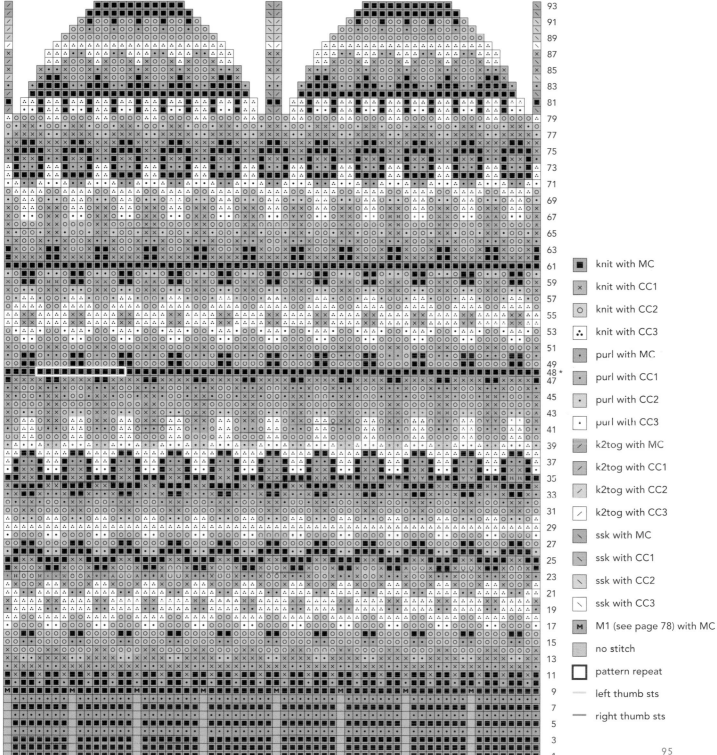

knit with MC
knit with CC1
knit with CC2
knit with CC3
purl with MC
purl with CC1
purl with CC2
purl with CC3
k2tog with MC
k2tog with CC1
k2tog with CC2
k2tog with CC3
ssk with MC
ssk with CC1
ssk with CC2
ssk with CC3
M1 (see page 78) with MC
no stitch
pattern repeat
left thumb sts
right thumb sts

* Work as given in directions

95

Thumb

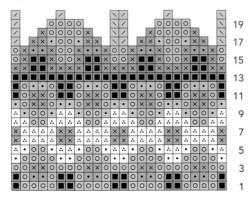

- ■ knit with MC
- ✕ knit with CC1
- ∩ knit with CC2
- ∴ knit with CC3
- • purl with CC1
- • purl with CC2
- • purl with CC3
- ╱ k2tog with CC2
- ╲ ssk with CC2
- ☐ pattern repeat

LEFT MITTEN: Work in patt to left thumb sts, place 11 thumb sts on holder, use the backward-loop method and MC to CO 11 sts over held sts, work in patt to end of rnd.

BOTH MITTENS: Work Rnds 49–93 of chart, dec as indicated—26 sts rem. Arrange the sts so that 13 front-of-hand sts are on 1 dpn and 13 back-of-hand sts are on a second dpn. Holding the needles parallel with WS facing tog, use the Kitchener st (see Glossary) to graft the sts tog.

Thumb

Pick up sts as foll.

RIGHT MITTEN: Transfer 11 held thumb sts onto dpn. With MC and RS facing, k11 thumb sts, pick up and knit 1 st at side of thumb opening and 11 sts along CO sts, pm to indicate beg of rnd (this is important for hand and thumb patts to match), and pick up and knit 1 st at other side of thumb opening—24 sts total.

LEFT MITTEN: Transfer 11 held thumb sts onto dpn. With MC and RS facing, k11 thumb sts, pick up and knit 1 st at side of thumb opening, 11 sts along CO sts, and 1 st at other side of thumb opening, pm to indicate beg of rnd—24 sts total.

BOTH MITTENS: Work Rnds 1–20 of Thumb chart—6 sts rem. Cut yarn, thread tail through rem sts, pull tight to close hole, and fasten off on WS. Weave in loose ends.

Lining

Remove waste yarn from provisional CO and carefully place exposed sts on smaller dpn—58 sts. Arrange sts as evenly as possible on 3 or 4 dpn, pm, and join for working in rnds. Work even in St st (knit every rnd) until piece measures 4½" (11.5 cm) from garter ridge at cuff.

Right Mitten

Knit to last 14 sts, place 9 sts on holder, use the backward-loop method to CO 9 sts over held sts, k5 to end of rnd.

Left Mitten

K5, place 9 sts on holder, use the backward-loop method to CO 9 sts over held sts, knit to end of rnd.

Both Mittens

Cont even until piece measures 8" (20.5 cm) from garter ridge at cuff. Weave in loose ends (see sidebar on page 94).

NEXT RND: K29, pm, knit to end.

DEC RND: *Ssk, knit to 2 sts before m, k2tog; rep from * once—4 sts dec'd.

Work 1 rnd even. Rep the last 2 rnds 3 more times—42 sts rem. Rep dec rnd every rnd 6 times—18 sts rem. Arrange the sts so that 9 front-of-hand sts are on 1 dpn and 9 back-of-hand sts are on a second dpn. Holding the needles parallel with WS facing tog, use the Kitchener st to graft the sts tog.

Thumb (both mittens)

Transfer 9 held thumb sts onto smaller dpn. With MC and RS facing, k9 thumb sts, pick up and knit 1 st at side of thumb opening and 9 sts along CO sts, pm, pick up and knit 1 st at other side of thumb opening—20 sts total. Work even in St st until thumb measures 1¾" (4.5 cm) from pick-up rnd.

NEXT RND: K10, pm, knit to end.

DEC RND: *Ssk, knit to 2 sts before m, k2tog; rep from * once—4 sts dec'd.

Rep dec rnd every rnd 2 more times—8 sts rem.

NEXT RND: *Ssk, k2tog; rep from * once—4 sts rem.

Cut yarn, thread tail through rem sts, pull tight to close hole, and fasten off on WS. Weave in loose ends.

BERET

With MC and smaller cir needle, CO 144 sts. Place marker (pm) and join for working in rnds, being careful not to twist sts. Work in k1, p1 rib until piece measures 1¼" (3.2 cm) from CO.

INC RND: *K2, k1f&b (see GLossary); rep from * to end—192 sts.

Change to larger cir needle. Work Rnds 1–66 of Beret chart, changing to dpn when necessary—8 sts rem.

Finishing

Cut yarn, thread tail through rem sts, pull tight to close hole, and fasten off on WS. Weave in loose ends. Block to measurements.

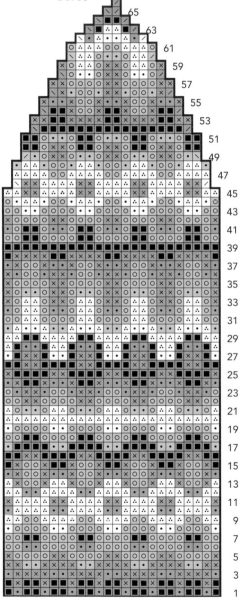

Beret

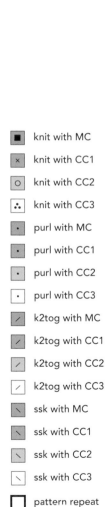

- ■ knit with MC
- × knit with CC1
- ○ knit with CC2
- ∴ knit with CC3
- • purl with MC
- • purl with CC1
- • purl with CC2
- • purl with CC3
- ╱ k2tog with MC
- ╱ k2tog with CC1
- ╱ k2tog with CC2
- ╱ k2tog with CC3
- ╲ ssk with MC
- ╲ ssk with CC1
- ╲ ssk with CC2
- ╲ ssk with CC3
- ☐ pattern repeat

Innsbruck
MITTENS + LEG WARMERS

DESIGNED BY COURTNEY KELLEY and
KATE GAGNON OSBORN

These mittens take their name from the capital of the western region of Austria, known as Tyrol, the other half of the historical Tyrolean region being Tirol in northern Italy. They feature twisted-stitch cables and embroidery in the style popularly referred to as Tyrolean knitting. The embroidered flowers on these mittens and leg warmers call to mind the wildflowers in bloom along the windswept Alps, which also inspired the intricately embroidered dirndl dresses that make up the historic women's costumes of the region. The embroidery, added in the spaces between the twisted stitches, is worked in a fingering-weight version of the yarn used to knit the pieces.

finished size
mittens: About 8" (20.5 cm) hand circumference and 9½" (24 cm) long from cuff to top of hand.

leg warmers: About 10½" (26.5 cm) leg circumference at widest point, unstretched, and 13½" (34.5 cm) long.

MATERIALS

yarn
Worsted weight (#4 Medium) for mittens and leg warmers; fingering weight (#1 Super Fine) for embroidery.

shown here: The Fibre Company Canopy Worsted (50% baby alpaca, 30% merino wool, 20% bamboo; 100 yd [91 m]/50 g): palm bud (pale blue; MC), 5 skeins. The Fibre Company Canopy Fingering (50% baby alpaca, 30% merino wool, 20% bamboo; 200 yd [183 m]/50 g): plum (CC1), cat's claw (yellow; CC2), and yerba mate (green; CC3), 1 skein each.

needles
mitten cuff: size U.S. 4 (3.5 mm): set of 5 double-pointed (dpn).

mitten hand: size U.S. 5 (3.75 mm): set of 5 dpn.

leg warmers: size U.S. 5 (3.75 mm): set of 5 dpn.

Adjust needle size if necessary to obtain the correct gauge.

notions
Markers (m); stitch holders or waste yarn; cable needle (cn); tapestry needle.

gauge
20 stitches and 30 rounds = 4" (10 cm) in stockinette stitch on larger needles, worked in rounds.

34 stitches and 30 rounds = 4" (10 cm) in twisted-stitch rib, unstretched, on larger needles, worked in rounds.

22 stitches and 33 rounds = 4" (10 cm) in twisted-stitch rib, stretched, on larger needles, worked in rounds.

Stitch Guide

Twisted Stitch Rib (multiple of 2 sts + 1)

ALL RNDS: *K1 through back loop (tbl), p1; rep from * to last st, k1tbl.

Left Dbl Dec

Sl 1 pwise, k2tog, psso—2 sts dec'd.

Right Dbl Dec

Ssk, sl 1 kwise, return 2 sts to left needle, pass second st on left needle over first, sl 1 pwise to right needle—2 sts dec'd.

Petal and Leaf Embroidery

Both mittens and leg warmers are finished with a petal and leaf embroidery pattern. The embroidery utilizes three techniques.

French Knot (worked in cat's claw)

1. Pull yarn through fabric from back to front, then wrap yarn around the needle 3 times.

2. Place needle back into fabric close to (but not in) the space you came up through.

3. Using both hands and holding the yarn in one and the needle in the other, pull the needle so that the yarn is tight.

Lazy Daisy Stitch (worked in plum for petals)

1. Pull yarn through fabric from back to front. Place needle back into fabric close to (but not in) the space you came up through, and bring needle back up to the front at the tip of desired petal placement, about ⅝" (1.5 cm) from entry point.

2. Wrap the yarn counterclockwise under the needle and pull taut.

3. Secure stitch by bringing needle back down into fabric, looping over the tip of petal.

Straight Stitch (worked in yerba mate for stem)

1. Pull yarn through fabric from back to front. Place needle back in fabric desired distance from entry point, then come up at beginning of next stitch (next to original entry point).

2. Repeat once more.

3. Place needle back into fabric and secure at back.

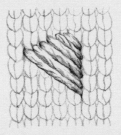

Right Mitten

With MC and smaller needles, CO 40 sts. Divide sts evenly over 4 dpn (10 sts per needle), place marker (pm), and join for working in rnds, being careful not to twist sts.

SET-UP RND: *P1, k2, p3, k1, p2, k2, p2, k1, p3, k2, p1; rep from *.

Cont in rib patt as established until piece measures 2½" (6.5 cm) from CO, or desired cuff length.

INC RND: *P1f&b (see Glossary), k2, p3, k1, p2, k2, p2, k1, p3, k2, p1f&b, pm; rep from *—44 sts.

Hand

Change to larger needles and work Rnd 1 of Mitten chart (see page 104) across 22 sts for back of hand, sl m, knit to end for palm. Work Rnd 2 of chart as established.

Shape Thumb Gusset

NEXT RND: (Rnd 3 of chart) Work in patt to m, sl m, k1f&b (see Glossary), pm, k21—2 gusset sts.

NEXT RND: Work in patt to m, knit to 1 st before next m, k1f&b, sl m, knit to end—1 st inc'd.

Rep last rnd 7 more times—10 gusset sts.

NEXT RND: (Rnd 12 of chart) Work in patt to m, place next 10 sts on holder to work later for thumb, remove m, use the backward-loop method (see Glossary) to CO 1 st over gap, knit to end—44 sts rem.

Upper Hand

Work even in patt through Rnd 38 of chart—piece measures about 8" (20.5 cm) from CO.

DEC RND: Work in patt to m, k1, ssk, knit to last 3 sts, k2tog, k1—4 sts dec'd.

Work 1 rnd even. Rep the last 2 rnds once more—36 sts rem. Rep dec rnd every rnd 7 times—8 sts rem.

Place 4 sts on each of 2 needles. Cut yarn, leaving a 12" (30.5 cm) tail. Thread tail on tapestry needle and use the Kitchener st (see Glossary) to graft sts tog.

	k1tbl
·	purl
	p2tog
	ssp
	sl 2 sts pwise, [sl 1 st to left needle by inserting left needle tip from right to left into st] 2 times, k2tog
	k2tog tbl
MP	M1 pwise (see Glossary)
	k1f&b (see Glossary)
	no stitch

	sl 1 st onto cn, hold in back, k1tbl, k1tbl from cn
	sl 1 st onto cn, hold in front, k1tbl, k1tbl from cn
	sl 1 st onto cn, hold in back, k1tbl, p1 from cn
	sl 1 st onto cn, hold in front, p1, k1tbl from cn

Mitten

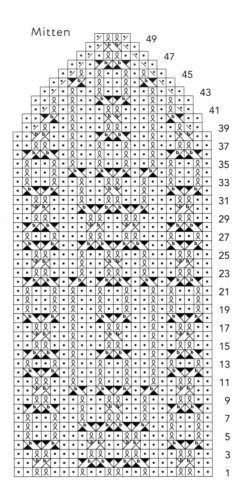

Leg Warmer

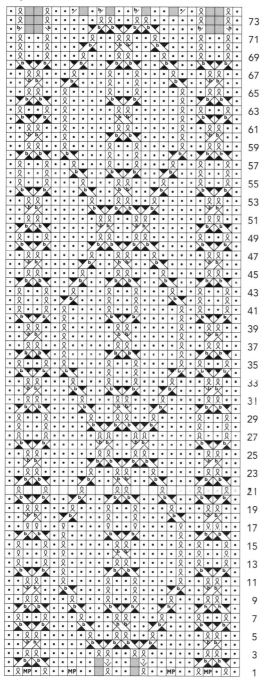

73
71
69
67
65
63
61
59
57
55
53
51
49
47
45
43
41
39
37
35
33
31
29
27
25
23
21
19
17
15
13
11
9
7
5
3
1

Thumb

Divide 10 held gusset sts evenly on 3 or 4 needles. Join MC and knit these 10 sts, then pick up and knit 2 sts at the base of the hand—12 sts total. Work even in St st until piece measures about 2" (5 cm) from pick-up rnd or ½" (1.3 cm) less than desired finished length. Dec as foll:

RND 1: *K2, k2tog; rep from *—9 sts rem.

RND 2: Knit.

RND 3: *K1, k2tog; rep from *—6 sts rem.

RND 4: *K2tog; rep from *—3 sts rem.

Cut yarn, thread tail through rem sts, pull tight to close hole, and fasten off on WS.

Finishing

Weave in loose ends. Following photo, add French knots, leaves, and stems as described on page 102.

Left Mitten

Work as for right mitten to beg of thumb gusset, ending with Rnd 2 of chart.

Shape Thumb Gusset

NEXT RND: (Rnd 3 of chart) Work in patt to m, sl m, k21, pm, k1f&b—2 gusset sts.

NEXT RND: Work in patt to m, sl m, knit to next m, sl m, k1f&b, knit to end—1 st inc'd.

Rep last rnd 7 more times—10 gusset sts.

NEXT RND: (Rnd 12 of chart) Work in patt to m, sl m, knit to next m, remove m, place next 10 sts on holder to work later for thumb, use the backward-loop method to CO 1 st over gap—44 sts rem.

Work upper hand, thumb, and finishing as for right mitten.

LEG WARMERS

With MC and larger needles, CO 73 sts. Divide sts as evenly as possible on 4 needles, place marker (pm), and join for working in rnds, being careful not to twist sts.

Ribbing

RNDS 1–12: [K1 through back loop (tbl), p1] 15 times, k1tbl, p4, k1tbl, p2, k1tbl, p4, [k1tbl, p1] 15 times.

RND 13: [K1tbl, p1] 13 times, k1tbl, pm, p1, k1tbl, p1, k1tbl, p4, k1tbl, p2, k1tbl, p4, k1tbl, p1, k1tbl, p1, pm, [k1tbl, p1] 13 times.

Leg

RNDS 1 AND 2: Work in twisted st rib (see Stitch Guide) to m, slip marker (sl m), work Leg Warmer chart to next m, sl m, work in twisted st rib to end—79 sts.

Work even in patt through Rnd 13 of chart.

DEC RND: K1tbl, p1, left dbl dec (see Stitch Guide), work in patt to last 4 sts, right dbl dec (see Stitch Guide), p1—4 sts dec'd.

Rep dec rnd every 11th rnd 5 more times—55 sts rem. Cont in patt through Rnd 74 of chart—47 sts rem.

Cuff

RNDS 1–13: *K1tbl, p1; rep from * to 1 st before m, k1tbl, sl m, p1, k2tbl, p4, k1tbl, p2, k1tbl, p4, k2tbl, p1, sl m, *k1tbl, p1; rep from * to end.

Loosely BO all sts in patt.

Finishing

Weave in loose ends. Steam-block to measurements. Embroider flower and leaf motifs as described on page 102.

WINTER HARBOR

WINTER SOMEHOW MAKES the ocean appear sharper as every rock, wave, and bit of foam is frozen in focus. The crisp air, blustery wind, and blue ocean blind our senses in the cold, brief moments of sunlight. As the days grow short and the nights fall quickly, the light glowing from the hearth warms the soul as family and friends gather. A beautiful icy harbor and a cup of strong black tea are all welcome reminders of winter's wonder.

This collection features a modern take on traditional coastal styles—soft as sea glass, but also stark and graphic like the winter sky against a rocky shore.

Traditional Aran, Fair Isle, and gansey sweaters with updated fit and construction, ocean-inspired motifs, and accessories designed to block out the winter chill are the cornerstones of this collection.

Taking inspiration from the sea and the night sky, this watery palette features blues, pale neutrals, deep charcoal grays, and seafoam green. Each sweater or accessory has a rugged look, but a definite feminine feel. They are meant to keep you comfortable throughout the long winter—pieces to layer while walking along a rocky coast on a crisp morning or warm sweaters to cuddle within while sitting by the fire.

Rhodes Point GANSEY

DESIGNED BY COURTNEY KELLEY

Named for a small town on Maryland's last inhabited island in the Chesapeake Bay, this pullover is inspired by the rich tradition of fishermen's ganseys. Traditionally a practical and hardwearing garment, this version has been updated to reflect a woman's touch. The yarn, a rich soft blend of alpaca, silk, cashmere, and camel, is a far cry from the lanolin-rich, gutsy wool sweaters of times past. The silhouette has been updated as well, but without sacrificing the worthwhile historical techniques. To provide a more feminine fit, I created a modified set-in sleeve that is shaped with short-rows at the underarm. An "invented" Channel Island bind-off for the cuffs combines Icelandic and picot bind-off methods and mirrors the cast-ons at the welts.

finished size
About 35¼ (36¾, 38½, 40, 41½, 43¼, 46½, 48, 49½, 51¼)" (89.5 [93.5, 98, 101.5, 105.5, 110, 118, 122, 125.5, 130] cm) bust circumference. Sweater shown measures 38½" (98 cm).

MATERIALS

yarn
Worsted weight (#4 Medium).

shown here: The Fibre Company Road to China (65% baby alpaca, 15% silk, 10% cashmere, 10% camel; 69 yd [63 m]/50 g): lapis, 15 (15, 16, 17, 19, 20, 25) skeins.

needles
body and sleeves: size U.S. 5 (3.75 mm): 16" and 24" (40 and 60 cm) circular (cir) and set of 4 or 5 double-pointed (dpn).

edging: size U.S. 3 (3.25 mm): 16" and 24" (40 and 60 cm) cir and set of 4 or 5 dpn.

Adjust needle size if necessary to obtain the correct gauge.

notions
Markers (m); stitch holders; tapestry needle.

gauge
20 stitches and 28 rounds = 4" (10 cm) in stockinette stitch on larger needle, worked in rounds.

Channel Island Cast-On

To begin, leave a tail of yarn that is about 2" (5 cm) long per stitch you are casting on. (For example, to cast on 10 stitches, leave a tail 20" [51 cm] long.) Fold this tail in half so that the yarn is doubled, make a slipknot near the open end of the folded tail and place the slipknot on the right-hand needle. There will be a strand of yarn attached to the ball as well as a short tail of yarn on one side of the slipknot and the double tail on the other side of the slipknot. Wrap the doubled tail counterclockwise twice around your left thumb, place the strand attached to the ball over your left index finger, and let the short tail hang free.

STEP 1. Bring the needle under the single strand on your index finger to make a yarnover (Figure 1).

STEP 2. Bring the needle up through the doubled strands on your thumb, grab a loop of the single strand as if to knit, then bring the needle back down through the loops on your thumb (Figure 2).

STEP 3. Release the wraps from your thumb and pull gently to snug up the stitch as you wrap the doubled tail counter-clockwise twice around your thumb in preparation to begin again—2 stitches have been cast on.

Repeat these 3 steps for the desired number of stitches, counting the slipknot for an odd number of stitches and omitting the slipknot for an even number of stitches.

Channel Island Bind-Off

STEP 1. *Insert tip of right-hand needle through first stitch on left-hand needle, leaving this stitch on the left-hand needle, then pull the second stitch on the left-hand needle through the first (Figure 1) and place it on the tip of the left-hand needle—the 2 stitches are crossed on the needle.

STEP 2. Knit the first of the crossed stitches and leave the old st on the needle (Figure 2).

STEP 3. Slip the new stitch onto the left-hand needle (Figure 3), and knit it again, then knit the next 2 stitches together (Figure 4).

STEP 4. Slip the second stitch on the right-hand needle over the first stitch (Figure 5) and off the needle to bind-off 1 stitch.

STEP 5. Return the remaining stitch to the left-hand needle.

Repeat these 5 steps for the desired number of stitches.

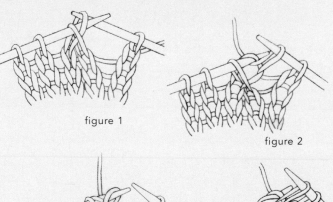

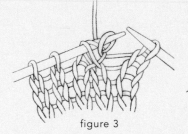

figure 1

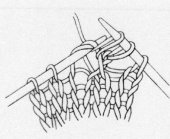

figure 2

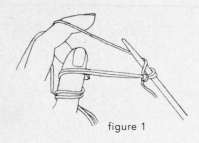

figure 1

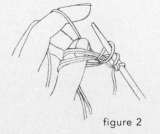

figure 2

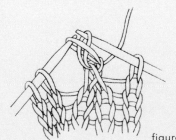

figure 3

figure 4

figure 5

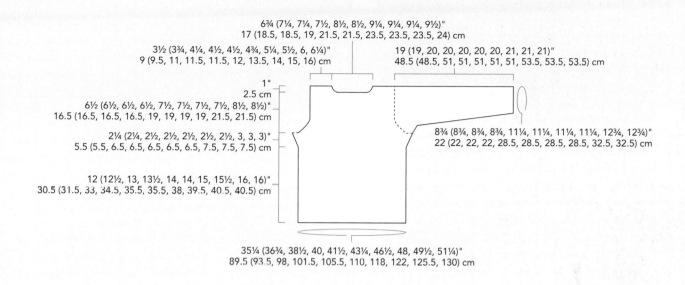

6¾ (7¼, 7¼, 7½, 8½, 8½, 9¼, 9¼, 9¼, 9½)"
17 (18.5, 18.5, 19, 21.5, 21.5, 23.5, 23.5, 23.5, 24) cm

3½ (3¾, 4¼, 4½, 4½, 4¾, 5¼, 5½, 6, 6¼)"
9 (9.5, 11, 11.5, 11.5, 12, 13.5, 14, 15, 16) cm

19 (19, 20, 20, 20, 20, 20, 21, 21, 21)"
48.5 (48.5, 51, 51, 51, 51, 51, 53.5, 53.5, 53.5) cm

1"
2.5 cm

6½ (6½, 6½, 6½, 7½, 7½, 7½, 7½, 8½, 8½)"
16.5 (16.5, 16.5, 16.5, 19, 19, 19, 19, 21.5, 21.5) cm

8¾ (8¾, 8¾, 8¾, 11¼, 11¼, 11¼, 11¼, 12¾, 12¾)"
22 (22, 22, 22, 28.5, 28.5, 28.5, 28.5, 32.5, 32.5) cm

2¼ (2¼, 2½, 2½, 2½, 2½, 2½, 3, 3, 3)"
5.5 (5.5, 6.5, 6.5, 6.5, 6.5, 6.5, 7.5, 7.5, 7.5) cm

12 (12½, 13, 13½, 14, 14, 15, 15½, 16, 16)"
30.5 (31.5, 33, 34.5, 35.5, 35.5, 38, 39.5, 40.5, 40.5) cm

35¼ (36¾, 38½, 40, 41½, 43¼, 46½, 48, 49½, 51¼)"
89.5 (93.5, 98, 101.5, 105.5, 110, 118, 122, 125.5, 130) cm

Body

Welts (make two)

With smaller, longer cir needle and using the Channel Island method (see sidebar at left), CO 88 (92, 96, 100, 104, 108, 116, 120, 124, 128) sts. Do not join. Work in garter st (knit every row) for 12 rows—6 garter ridges.

Join Welts

With larger, longer cir needle and RS facing, knit across first welt, place marker (pm) to denote side seam, knit across second welt—176 (184, 192, 200, 208, 216, 232, 240, 248, 256) sts total. Pm to denote other side seam and beg of rnd and join for working in rnds, being careful not to twist sts.

NEXT RND: P1, knit to 1 st before m, p1, slip marker (sl m), p1, knit to 1 st before next m, p1.

Rep this rnd 5 more times—6 rnds total.

Optional Initials

SET-UP RND: K12, pm, work initials as desired according to Alphabet chart (see page 114), pm, work to end of rnd.

Following Alphabet chart and purling 2 sts at each side as established, cont in patt to end of Alphabet chart. Remove chart markers. Work even in St st with purl sts at each side until piece measures 12 (12½, 13, 13½, 14, 14, 15, 15½, 16, 16)" (30.5 [31.5, 33, 34.5, 35.5, 35.5, 38, 39.5, 40.5, 40.5] cm) from CO or desired length to underarm gusset.

Alphabet

□ k on RS; p on WS

• p on RS; k on WS

Shape Underarm Gusset

RND 1: *P1, knit to 1 st before next m, p1, pm, M1 (see page 78), sl m; rep from * once more—2 sts inc'd.

RND 2: *P1, knit to 1 st before next m, p1, sl m, k1, sl m; rep from * once more.

RND 3: *P1, knit to 1 st before next m, p1, sl m, M1, knit to next m, M1, sl m; rep from * once more—4 sts inc'd.

RNDS 4 AND 5: *P1, knit to 1 st before next m, p1, sl m, knit to next m; rep from * once more.

Rep the last 3 rnds 3 (3, 4, 4, 4, 4, 4, 5, 5, 5) more times—11 (11, 13, 13, 13, 13, 13, 15, 15, 15) sts in each gusset worked as foll: P1, k9 (9, 11, 11, 11, 11, 11, 13, 13, 13), p1.

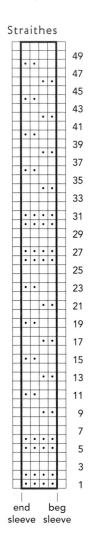

Straithes

□ k on RS; p on WS

· p on RS; k on WS

□ pattern repeat

end sleeve   beg sleeve

Divide for Front and Back

NEXT RND: P1, knit to 1 st before next m, p1, k9 (9, 11, 11, 11, 11, 11, 13, 13, 13), p1 and place these 11 (11, 13, 13, 13, 13, 13, 15, 15, 15) sts on holder for gusset (remove markers), knit to 1 st before next m and place these 86 (90, 94, 98, 102, 106, 114, 118, 122, 126) sts on holder for back, p1, k9 (9, 11, 11, 11, 11, 11, 13, 13, 13), p1 (first st of next rnd) and place these 11 (11, 13, 13, 13, 13, 13, 15, 15, 15) sts on holder for gusset—86 (90, 94, 98, 102, 106, 114, 118, 122, 126) sts rem for front.

Front

Note: Chart beg before armhole shaping ends; read the foll section all the way through before proceeding.

Working front sts back and forth in rows, shape armhole as foll:

DEC ROW: (RS) Work 3 sts in garter st, work 1 st in rev St st (purl on RS; knit on WS), pm, ssk, work to last 6 sts, k2tog, pm, work 1 st in rev St st, work 3 sts in garter st—2 sts dec'd.

Rep dec row every RS row 7 more times—70 (74, 78, 82, 86, 90, 98, 102, 106, 110) sts rem. *At the same time* when piece measures 0 (0, 0, 0, 1, 1, 1, 1, 2, 2)" (0 [0, 0, 0, 2.5, 2.5, 2.5, 2.5, 5, 5] cm) from dividing row, ending with a WS row, work Rows 1–50 of Straithes chart between markers, then work Rows 1–6 once more—piece measures 6½ (6½, 6½, 6½, 7½, 7½, 7½, 7½, 8½, 8½)" (16.5 [16.5, 16.5, 16.5, 19, 19, 19, 19, 21.5, 21.5] cm) from dividing row.

Shape Neck

K22 (23, 25, 26, 26, 28, 30, 32, 34, 35), place next 26 (28, 28, 30, 34, 34, 38, 38, 38, 40) sts on holder for neck, join new yarn and knit to end—22 (23, 25, 26, 26, 28, 30, 32, 34, 35) sts rem each side. Working each side separately in garter st, dec 1 st at each neck edge every RS row 4 times as foll:

DEC ROW: (RS) Knit to 3 sts before neck edge, k2tog, k1; on second side, k1, ssk, knit to end—1 st dec'd each side; 18 (19, 21, 22, 22, 24, 26, 28, 30, 31) sts rem each side when all decs have been completed.

Place sts on holders.

Back

Return 86 (90, 94, 98, 102, 106, 114, 118, 122, 126) held back sts onto larger needle. Work as for front, omitting neck shaping and ending with Row 6 of chart. Leave sts on needle.

Join Shoulders

Place 18 (19, 21, 22, 22, 24, 26, 28, 30, 31) held left front sts onto a second needle. With WS facing tog, use the three-needle method (see Glossary) to join left front sts tog with corresponding 18 (19, 21, 22, 22, 24, 26, 28, 30, 31) back sts for left shoulder. Rep for right shoulder. Place rem 34 (36, 36, 38, 42, 42, 46, 46, 46, 48) back sts on a holder.

Sleeves

With larger, shorter cir needle or dpn, RS facing, and beg after held gusset sts, pick up and knit 60 (60, 60, 60, 72, 72, 72, 72, 80, 80) sts evenly spaced around armhole, pm, then work gusset sts as: p1, k9 (9, 11, 11, 11, 11, 11, 13, 13, 13), p1, pm to denote beg of rnd. Work short-rows (see page 70) as foll:

SHORT-ROW 1: (RS) K8, wrap next st, turn work.

SHORT-ROW 2: (WS) Sl 1, k7, sl m, k1, purl to 1 st before m, k1, sl m, k8, wrap next st, turn work.

SHORT-ROW 3: Sl 1, k7, sl m, p1, ssk, knit to 3 sts before m, k2tog, p1, sl m, k6, wrap next st, turn work—2 gusset sts dec'd.

SHORT-ROW 4: Sl 1, k5, sl m, k1, purl to 1 st before m, k1, sl m, k6, wrap next st, turn work.

SHORT-ROW 5: Sl 1, k5, sl m, p1, knit to 1 st before m, p1, sl m, k4, wrap next st, turn work.

SHORT-ROW 6: Sl 1, k3, sl m, k1, p2tog, purl to 3 sts before m, ssp (see Glossary), k1, sl m, k4, wrap next st, turn work—2 gusset sts dec'd.

SHORT-ROW 7: Sl 1, k3, sl m, p1, knit to 1 st before m, p1, sl m, k2, wrap next st, turn work.

SHORT-ROW 8: Sl 1, k1, sl m, k1, purl to 1 st before m, k1, sl m, k2, wrap next st, turn work.

NEXT ROW: Sl 1, k1, sl m, p1, ssk, knit to 3 sts before m, k2tog, p1—2 gusset sts dec'd.

NEXT RND: Knit to m, working wraps tog with wrapped sts as you come to them, sl m, p1, knit to 1 st before m, p1.

SET-UP RND: Beg and ending as indicated for sleeve, work Rnd 1 of Straithes chart to m, sl m, p1, knit to 1 st before m, p1.

Work 0 (0, 3, 3, 3, 3, 3, 6, 6, 6) rnds in patt and *at the same time* dec 2 gusset sts every 3rd rnd as established—5 gusset sts rem.

NEXT RND: Work Rnd 2 (2, 5, 5, 5, 5, 5, 8, 8, 8) of chart to m, sl m, p1, sl 1, k2tog, psso, p1—3 gusset sts rem.

NEXT RND: Work Rnd 3 (3, 6, 6, 6, 6, 6, 9, 9, 9) of chart to m, sl m, p2tog, p1—62 (62, 62, 62, 74, 74, 74, 74, 82, 82) sts rem.

Work even in patt through Rnd 31 of chart, purling 2 gusset sts throughout. Change to St st, keeping 2 purl sts as established, and work even for 2 (2, 2, 2, 2½, 2½, 2½, 2½, 3, 3)" (5 [5, 5, 5, 6.5, 6.5, 6.5, 6.5, 7.5, 7.5] cm).

DEC RND: K1, k2tog, knit to 3 sts before m, ssk, k1, sl m, p2—2 sts dec'd.

Rep dec rnd every 8th rnd 8 more times—44 (44, 44, 44, 56, 56, 56, 56, 64, 64) sts rem. Work even until piece measures 18 (18, 19, 19, 19, 19, 19, 20, 20, 20)" (45.5 [45.5, 48.5, 48.5, 48.5, 48.5, 48.5, 51, 51, 51] cm) from pick-up rnd at shoulder, or 1" (2.5 cm) less than desired finished length. [Purl 1 rnd, knit 1 rnd] 4 times, then purl 1 rnd. Using the Channel Island method (see sidebar on page 112), BO all sts.

Finishing

Weave in loose ends. Block to measurements.

Neckband

With smaller, shorter cir needle and RS facing, k26 (28, 28, 30, 34, 34, 38, 38, 38, 40) held front neck sts, pick up and knit 4 sts over 8 rows of neck shaping, k34 (36, 36, 38, 42, 42, 46, 46, 46, 48) held back neck sts, pick up and knit 4 sts over 8 rows of neck shaping—68 (72, 72, 76, 84, 84, 92, 92, 92, 96) sts total. Pm and join for working in rnds. Work in k2, p2 rib for 1½" (3.8 cm), then work 4 rnds in St st. BO all sts.

Telemark
LEG WARMERS

DESIGNED BY KATE GAGNON OSBORN

Norwegian folk costume—bold graphics from Fana, iconic lice-stitch patterns from the Setesdal valley, and Selbu mittens and accessories—comprise most of what we view as traditional Norwegian knitting. The bold geometrics in Fana garments, popular in black or brown and white during the late nineteenth and early twentieth centuries, originated as part of men's traditional costume. The lice-patterned sweaters from the Setesdal valley—white patterning and geometric color-work against a black background—can be traced back to the 1840s. Selbu knitting originated with a pair of black-on-white patterned mittens knitted by a young girl in the mid-1800s. All three of these traditional components—graphic motifs, lice patterning, and black-on-white colorwork—are united in this pair of contemporary leg warmers.

MATERIALS

yarn
Worsted weight (#4 Medium).

shown here: The Fibre Company Canopy Worsted (50% baby alpaca, 30% merino wool, 20% bamboo; 100 yd [91 m]/50 g): orchid (MC), 3 skeins; obsidian (CC), 1 skein.

needles
leg: size U.S. 7 (4.5 mm): set of 4 or 5 double-pointed (dpn).

edging: size U.S. 5 (3.75 mm): set of 4 or 5 dpn.

Adjust needle size if necessary to obtain the correct gauge.

notions
Marker (m); tapestry needle.

gauge
22 stitches and 26 rounds = 4" (10 cm) in leg pattern on larger needles, worked in rounds.

finished size
About 11" (28 cm) circumference at cuff, 14½" (37 cm) circumference at knee, and 17¼" (44 cm) overall length.

Sewn Bind-Off

A tight ribbing at the top of the leg is crucial for these leg warmers to stay in place. Instead of using a standard bind-off at the top of the leg (which might prevent the leg warmers from stretching enough to get on or fit comfortably), the sewn bind-off is used. This bind-off, first introduced by the inimitable Elizabeth Zimmermann, guarantees an elastic edge and a comfortable fit.

To work this bind off, cut a tail three times the circumference of your work—about 45" (114.5 cm) in this case. Thread the tail on a tapestry needle and work as follows:

*Bring the tapestry needle through the first two stitches purlwise (Figure 1) and pull the yarn through, then bring the tapestry needle through the first stitch knitwise (Figure 2) and pull the yarn through, then slip the first stitch off the needle. Repeat from * to the end of the stitches to be bound off. To finish, bring the tapestry needle purlwise through the remaining stitch and fasten off.

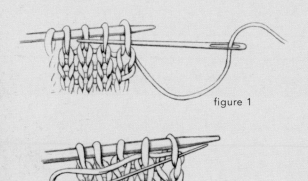

figure 1

figure 2

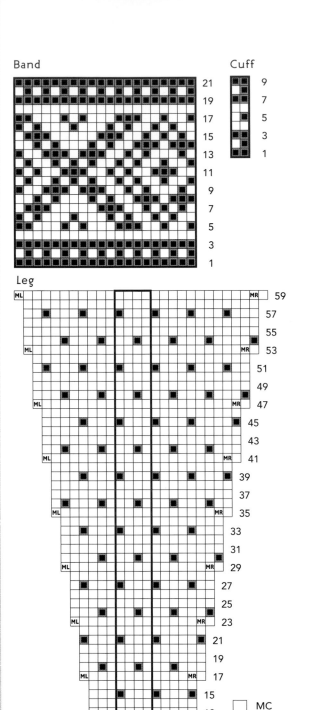

Band

Cuff

Leg

MC

CC

M1R (see page 78)

M1L (see page 78)

pattern repeat

Leg Warmer

With MC and smaller needles, CO 56 sts. Arrange sts as evenly as possible on 3 or 4 dpn, place marker (pm), and join for working in rnds, being careful not to twist sts. Work in k1, p1 rib until piece measures 1" (2.5 cm) from CO.

INC RND: *K14, M1 (see page 78); rep from *—60 sts.

Change to larger needles. Work Rnds 1–9 of Cuff chart.

Work Rnds 1–59 of Leg chart, inc as indicated on chart—80 sts.

Work Rnds 1–21 of Band chart—piece measures about 15¾" (40 cm) from CO. With MC, knit 1 rnd.

DEC RND: *K8, k2tog; rep from *—72 sts rem.

Change to smaller needles. Work in k1, p1 rib for 1½" (3.8 cm). Using the sewn method (see sidebar at left), BO all sts.

Finishing

Weave in loose ends. Block to measurements.

Erin CARDIGAN

DESIGNED BY KATE GAGNON OSBORN

Cabled Aran sweaters—named for the islands off the coast of Ireland where they are believed to have originated—are ubiquitous, but surprisingly recent additions to knitwear history. They became widespread in the early 1900s when women of the islands began to knit garments to supplement sparse household income; patterns became commercially available in the 1940s. Of the many myths surrounding these sweaters, one of the most widespread is that a fisherman drowned at sea could be identified by the unique pattern of his sweater. What is established fact is that as knitting trends change and evolve, Aran sweaters continue to be hugely popular. This sweater, while heavily inspired by tradition, has been updated with set-in sleeves, saddle shoulders, and a more figure-flattering fit.

MATERIALS

yarn
Sportweight (#2 Fine).

shown here: The Fibre Company Savannah (50% wool, 20% cotton, 15% linen, 15% soy fiber; 160 yd [146 m]/50 g): chambray, 9 (10, 12, 13, 15, 15) skeins.

needles
body and sleeves: size U.S. 6 (4 mm).

ribbing: size U.S. 4 (3.5 mm).

Adjust needle size if necessary to obtain the correct gauge.

notions
Markers (m); cable needle (cn); tapestry needle; twelve ½" (1.3 cm) buttons.

gauge
21 stitches and 35 rows = 4" (10 cm) in seed stitch on larger needles.

Center sleeve cable panel (Sleeve Chart B) = 2¼" (5.5 cm) wide.

Main back cable panel (Chart D) = 4¾" (12 cm) wide.

finished size
About 31 (35½, 40, 43, 47½, 50½)" (78.5 [90, 101.5, 109, 120.5, 128.5] cm) bust circumference; designed for a close fit with zero ease. Sweater shown measures 35½" (90 cm).

Stitch Guide

Seed Stitch (multiple of 2 sts)

ROW 1: *P1, k1; rep from *.

ROW 2: Purl the knits and knit the purls.

Rep Row 2 for patt.

Measuring Gauge on Cable Patterns

Sweaters designed with a lot of cabling are easy to knit once the proper gauge has been achieved. Because many sweaters incorporate multiple cable patterns and because the gauge in each pattern can differ, it is a good idea to measure the gauge in the given filler stitch (seed stitch for this pattern) as well as in the cable patterns. This process takes just a little bit longer than swatching a single stitch pattern, but it ensures the best possible end result—and is arguably much quicker than ripping out an entire ill-fitting sweater!

To measure the gauge properly, simply isolate a few of the main cable patterns in the garment and knit a swatch for each cable pattern, plus a few extra stitches on each side for ease in measuring gauge. Knit a full pattern repeat, then block the swatch and measure the width of the cable repeat. For example, the larger main cable pattern in this pattern is 34 stitches wide and measures 4¾" (12 cm) wide, or 7.16 stitches per inch (2.5 cm).

Back

With smaller needles, CO 82 (94, 106, 114, 126, 134) sts.

SET UP ribbing: (RS) K1, [p1, k1] 1 (4, 7, 9, 12, 14) time(s), place marker (pm), *work 8 sts according to Ribbing Chart A (see page 128), pm, work 12 sts according to Ribbing Chart B, pm, work 8 sts according to Ribbing Chart A, pm*, work 20 sts according to Ribbing Chart D, pm, rep from * to * once, [k1, p1] 1 (4, 7, 9, 12, 14) time(s), k1.

Work in rib as established until piece measures 2½" (6.5 cm) from CO, ending with a WS row. Change to larger needles.

INC ROW: (RS) K1, [p1, k1] 1 (4, 7, 9, 12, 14) time(s), slip marker (sl m), *work Row 1 of Ribbing Increase Chart A, sl m, work Row 1 of Body Ribbing Increase Chart B, sl m, work Row 1 of Ribbing Increase Chart A, sl m*, work Row 1 of Ribbing Increase Chart D, rep from * to * once, [p1, k1] 1 (4, 7, 9, 12, 14) time(s), k1—102 (114, 126, 134, 146, 154) sts.

Keeping edge sts in St st and maintaining seed st (see Stitch Guide) on each side of cables as established (i.e., purl the knits and knit the purls), work through Row 6 of charts—120 (132, 144, 152, 164, 172) sts.

SET-UP ROW: (RS) K1, [p1, k1] 1 (4, 7, 9, 12, 14) time(s), sl m, *work Row 1 of Chart A, sl m, work Row 1 of Body Chart B, sl m, work Row 1 of Chart A, sl m*, work Row 1 of Chart D, sl m, rep from * to * once, [p1, k1] 1 (4, 7, 9, 12, 14) time(s), k1.

Work in patts as established until piece measures 16 (16, 16½, 16½, 17, 17)" (40.5 [40.5, 42, 42, 43, 43] cm) from CO or desired length to underarm, ending with a WS row.

Shape Armholes

Cont in patt, BO 4 (5, 5, 6, 6, 7) sts at beg of next 2 rows, then BO 2 (3, 4, 5, 6, 6) sts at beg of foll 2 rows, then BO 0 (0, 0, 0, 4, 5) sts at beg of foll 0 (0, 0, 0, 2, 2) rows—108 (116, 126, 130, 132, 136) sts rem. Dec 1 st each end of needle every RS row 4 (6, 8, 9, 9, 10) times, then every 4th row 3 (4, 4, 4, 4, 5) times—94 (96, 102, 104, 106, 106) sts rem. Work in patt until armholes measure 6¼ (6¾, 7¼, 7½, 8, 8¼)" (16 [17, 18.5, 19, 20.5, 21] cm), ending with a WS row.

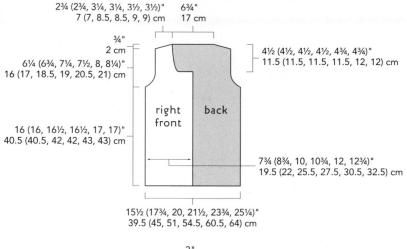

2¾ (2¾, 3¼, 3¼, 3½, 3½)"
7 (7, 8.5, 8.5, 9, 9) cm

6¾"
17 cm

¾"
2 cm

4½ (4½, 4½, 4½, 4¾, 4¾)"
11.5 (11.5, 11.5, 11.5, 12, 12) cm

6¼ (6¾, 7¼, 7½, 8, 8¼)"
16 (17, 18.5, 19, 20.5, 21) cm

right front

back

16 (16, 16½, 16½, 17, 17)"
40.5 (40.5, 42, 42, 43, 43) cm

7¾ (8¾, 10, 10¾, 12, 12¾)"
19.5 (22, 25.5, 27.5, 30.5, 32.5) cm

15½ (17¾, 20, 21½, 23¾, 25¼)"
39.5 (45, 51, 54.5, 60.5, 64) cm

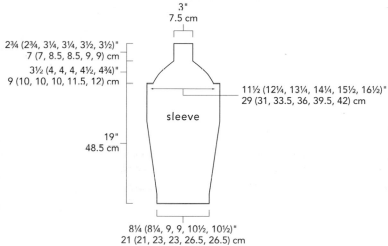

3"
7.5 cm

2¾ (2¾, 3¼, 3¼, 3½, 3½)"
7 (7, 8.5, 8.5, 9, 9) cm

3½ (4, 4, 4, 4½, 4¾)"
9 (10, 10, 10, 11.5, 12) cm

11½ (12¼, 13¼, 14¼, 15½, 16½)"
29 (31, 33.5, 36, 39.5, 42) cm

sleeve

19"
48.5 cm

8¼ (8¼, 9, 9, 10½, 10½)"
21 (21, 23, 23, 26.5, 26.5) cm

Shape Shoulders

BO 7 (8, 9, 10, 10, 10) sts at beg of next 2 rows, then BO 7 (7, 8, 9, 10, 11) sts at beg of foll 2 rows—66 (66, 68, 66, 66, 64) sts rem. BO 7 (7, 8, 7, 7, 6) sts at beg of next 2 rows—52 sts rem. BO all sts.

Right Front

With smaller needles, CO 41 (47, 53, 57, 63, 67) sts.

SET UP RIBBING: (RS) K1, p1, pm, work 8 sts according to Ribbing Chart C, pm, work 8 sts according to Ribbing Chart A, pm, work 12 sts according to Ribbing Chart B, pm, work 8 sts according to Ribbing Chart A, pm, [k1, p1] 1 (4, 7, 9, 12, 14) time(s), k1.

Work in rib as established until piece measures 2½" (6.5 cm) from CO, ending with a WS row. Change to larger needles.

INC ROW: (RS) K1, p1, sl m, work Row 1 of Ribbing Increase Chart C, sl m, work Row 1 of Ribbing Increase Chart A, sl m,

Chart A

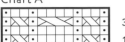

3

1

Body Chart B

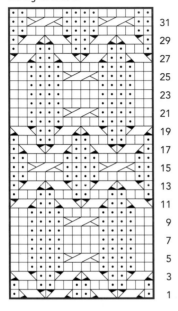

31
29
27
25
23
21
19
17
15
13
11
9
7
5
3
1

Chart C

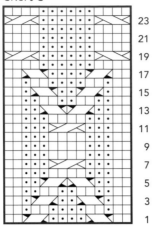

23
21
19
17
15
13
11
9
7
5
3
1

Ribbing Chart A

1

Ribbing Chart B

1

Ribbing Chart C

1

Ribbing Chart D

1

Chart D

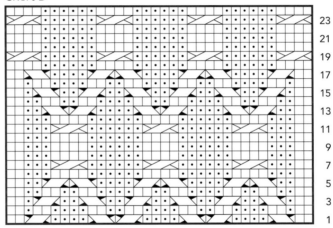

23
21
19
17
15
13
11
9
7
5
3
1

Ribbing Increase Chart A

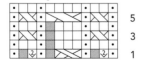

5

3

1

Body Ribbing Increase Chart B

5

3

1

Ribbing Increase Chart C

5

3

1

Ribbing Increase Chart D

5

3

1

Sleeve Chart B

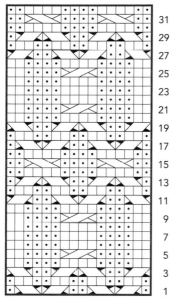

31
29
27
25
23
21
19
17
15
13
11
9
7
5
3
1

Sleeve Ribbing Increase Chart B

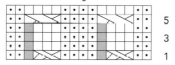

5
3
1

☐ k on RS; p on WS

· p on RS; k on WS

MP M1 pwise (see Glossary)

↓ k1f&b (see Glossary)

▨ no stitch

☐ pattern repeat

sl 1 st onto cn, hold in front, k1, k1 from cn

sl 1 st onto cn, hold in back, k1, k1f&b from cn

sl 1 st onto cn, hold in front, k1f&b, k1 from cn

sl 1 st onto cn, hold in back, k2, p1 from cn

sl 2 sts onto cn, hold in front, p1, k2 from cn

sl 1 st onto cn, hold in back, k2, k1f&b from cn

sl 2 sts onto cn, hold in front, k1f&b, k2 from cn

sl 2 sts onto cn, hold in back, k2, k2 from cn

sl 2 sts onto cn, hold in front, k2, k2 from cn

work Row 1 of Body Ribbing Increase Chart B, sl m, work Row 1 of Ribbing Increase Chart A, sl m, [p1, k1] 1 (4, 7, 9, 12, 14) time(s), k1—51 (57, 63, 67, 73, 77) sts.

Keeping edge sts in St st and maintaining seed st at side edge as established, work through Row 6 of increase charts—59 (65, 71, 75, 81, 85) sts.

SET-UP ROW: (RS) K1, p1, sl m, work Row 1 of Chart C, sl m, work Row 1 of Chart A, sl m, work Row 1 of Body Chart B, sl m, work Row 1 of Chart A, sl m, work in seed st as established to last st, k1.

Cont in patts as established until piece measures same as back to underarm, ending with a RS row.

Shape Armhole

Note: Neck shaping beg while armhole shaping is in progress; read all the way through the next sections before proceeding.

With WS facing and cont in patt, BO 4 (5, 5, 6, 6, 7) sts at armhole edge (beg of WS rows) once, then BO 2 (3, 4, 5, 6, 6) sts once, then BO 0 (0, 0, 0, 4, 5) sts once—53 (57, 62, 64, 65, 67) sts rem. Dec 1 st at armhole edge every RS row 4 (6, 8, 9, 9, 10) times, then every 4th row 3 (4, 4, 4, 4, 5) times. *At the same time* when armhole measures 2½ (3, 3½, 3¾, 4, 4¼)" (6.5 [7.5, 9, 9.5, 10, 11] cm), shape neck as foll.

Shape Neck

Cont working armhole shaping as established, at neck edge (beg of RS rows), BO 18 sts once, then BO 2 sts 2 times. Dec 1 st at neck edge every RS row 3 times—21 (22, 25, 26, 27, 27) sts rem after all neck and armhole shaping is complete. Work even in patt until armhole measures 6¼ (6¾, 7¼, 7½, 8, 8¼)" (16 [17, 18.5, 19, 20.5, 21] cm), ending with a RS row.

Shape Shoulder

At armhole edge (beg of WS rows), BO 7 (8, 9, 10, 10, 10) sts once, then BO 7 (7, 8, 9, 10, 11) sts once—7 (7, 8, 7, 7, 6) sts rem. At beg of next WS row, BO all sts.

INC ROW: (RS) K1, [p1, k1] 1 (4, 7, 9, 12, 14) time(s), sl m, work Row 1 of Ribbing Increase Chart A, sl m, work Row 1 of Body Ribbing Increase Chart B, sl m, work Row 1 of Ribbing Increase Chart A, sl m, work Row 1 of Ribbing Increase Chart C, sl m, p1, k1—51 (57, 63, 67, 73, 77) sts.

Keeping edge sts in St st and maintaining seed st at side edge as established, work through Row 6 of increase charts—59 (65, 71, 75, 81, 85) sts.

SET-UP ROW: (RS) K1, work in seed st as established to m, sl m, work Row 1 of Chart A, sl m, work Row 1 of Body Chart B, sl m, work Row 1 of Chart A, sl m, work Row 1 of Chart C, sl m, p1, k1.

Cont in patts as established until piece measures same as back to underarm, ending with a WS row.

Shape Armhole

Note: Neck shaping beg while armhole shaping is in progress; read all the way through the next sections before proceeding.

With RS facing and cont in patt, BO 4 (5, 5, 6, 6, 7) sts at armhole edge (beg of RS rows) once, then BO 2 (3, 4, 5, 6, 6) sts once, then BO 0 (0, 0, 0, 4, 5) sts once—53 (57, 62, 64, 65, 67) sts rem. Dec 1 st at armhole edge every RS row 4 (6, 8, 9, 9, 10) times, then every 4th row 3 (4, 4, 4, 4, 5) times. *At the same time* when armhole measures 2½ (3, 3½, 3¾, 4, 4¼)" (6.5 [7.5, 9, 9.5, 10, 11] cm), shape neck as foll.

Shape Neck

Cont working armhole shaping as established, at neck edge (beg of WS rows), BO 18 sts once, then BO 2 sts 2 times. Dec 1 st at neck edge every RS row 3 times—21 (22, 25, 26, 27, 27) sts rem after all neck and armhole shaping is complete. Work even in patt until armhole measures 6¼ (6¾, 7¼, 7½, 8, 8¼)" (16 [17, 18.5, 19, 20.5, 21] cm), ending with a WS row.

Shape Shoulder

At armhole edge (beg of RS rows), BO 7 (8, 9, 10, 10, 10) sts once, then BO 7 (7, 8, 9, 10, 11) sts once—7 (7, 8, 7, 7, 6) sts rem. At beg of next RS row, BO all sts.

Left Front

With smaller needles, CO 41 (47, 53, 57, 63, 67) sts.

SET UP RIBBING: (RS) K1, [p1, k1] 1 (4, 7, 9, 12, 14) time(s), pm, work 8 sts according to Ribbing Chart A, pm, work 12 sts according to Ribbing Chart B, pm, work 8 sts according to Ribbing Chart A, pm, work 8 sts according to Ribbing Chart C, pm, p1, k1.

Work in rib as established until piece measures 2½" (6.5 cm) from CO, ending with a WS row. Change to larger needles.

Sleeves

With smaller needles, CO 46 (46, 50, 50, 58, 58) sts.

SET UP RIBBING: (RS) K1, [p1, k1] 4 (4, 5, 5, 7, 7) times, pm, work 8 sts according to Ribbing Chart A, pm, work 12 sts according to Ribbing Chart B, pm, work 8 sts according to Ribbing Chart A, pm, [k1, p1] 4 (4, 5, 5, 7, 7) times, k1.

Work in rib as established until piece measures 1½" (3.8 cm) from CO, ending with a WS row. Change to larger needles.

INC ROW: (RS) K1, [p1, k1] 4 (4, 5, 5, 7, 7) times, sl m, work Row 1 of Ribbing Increase Chart A, sl m, work Row 1 of Sleeve Ribbing Increase Chart B, sl m, work Row 1 of Ribbing Increase Chart A, sl m, [p1, k1] 4 (4, 5, 5, 7, 7) times, k1—54 (54, 58, 58, 66, 66) sts.

Keeping edge sts in St st and maintaining seed st at each edge as established, work through Row 6 of increase charts—58 (58, 62, 62, 70, 70) sts.

SET UP ROW: (RS) K1, [p1, k1] 4 (4, 5, 5, 7, 7) times, sl m, work Row 1 of Chart A, sl m, work Row 1 of Sleeve Chart B, sl m, work Row 1 of Chart A, sl m, [p1, k1] 4 (4, 5, 5, 7, 7) times, k1.

Working in patt as established, inc 1 st each end of needle every 8th row 9 (11, 11, 14, 13, 16) times, working new sts into seed st patt—76 (80, 84, 90, 96, 102) sts. Cont even in patt until piece measures 19" (48.5 cm) from CO or desired length to underarm, ending with a WS row.

Shape Cap

With RS facing and cont in patt, BO 5 (5, 5, 5, 5, 6) sts at beg of next 2 rows, then BO 3 (3, 3, 4, 4, 4) sts at beg of foll 2 rows, then BO 2 (2, 2, 3, 3, 3) sts at beg of foll 2 rows—56 (60, 64, 66, 72, 76) sts rem. Dec 1 st each end of needle every row 0 (0, 2, 4, 6, 8) times, then every other row 8 (10, 10, 9, 10, 10) times as foll: on RS rows, k1, ssk, work in patt to last 3 sts, k2tog, k1; on WS rows, p1, p2tog, work in patt to last 3 sts, ssp (see Glossary), p1—2 sts dec'd each dec row; 40 sts rem after all decs have been worked. BO 2 sts at beg of next 4 rows, then BO 3 sts at beg of foll 4 rows—20 sts rem.

Saddle

NEXT ROW: (RS) K1, p1, work according to Sleeve Chart B to last 2 sts, p1, k1. Work in patt as established, working the edge sts in St st and the adjoining sts in rev St st (purl on RS; knit on WS), until saddle measures 2¾ (2¾, 3¼, 3¼, 3½, 3½)" (7 [7, 8.5, 8.5, 9, 9] cm) or same length as shoulder width. BO all sts.

Finishing

Gently steam-press all pieces to measurements. With yarn threaded on a tapestry needle, sew front sleeve cap into front armhole, then sew each saddle strap to front and back shoulder, then sew back sleeve cap into back armhole. Sew sleeve and side seams.

Buttonband

With smaller needles and RS facing, pick up and knit 95 (97, 102, 104, 107, 108) sts evenly spaced along center left front edge. Work in seed st until band measures 1" (2.5 cm) from pick-up row. BO all sts in patt. Mark placement of 11 buttons, one ½" (1.3 cm) up from CO edge, one 1" (2.5 cm) below neck edge, and the others evenly spaced in between.

Buttonhole Band

With smaller needles and RS facing, pick up and knit 95 (97, 102, 104, 107, 108) sts evenly spaced along center right front edge. Work in seed st until band measures ½" (1.3 cm) from pick-up row, ending with a WS row.

BUTTONHOLE ROW: (RS) Keeping in patt, work 2-st 1-row buttonhole (see Glossary) opposite each button marker.

Work in patt until band measures 1" (2.5 cm) from pick-up row. BO all sts in patt.

Neckband

With smaller needles and RS facing, pick up and knit 127 sts evenly spaced along neck edge. Work in seed st until band measures ¾" (2 cm) from pick-up row, ending with a WS row.

BUTTONHOLE ROW: (RS) Keeping in patt, work 2-st 1-row buttonhole aligned with those on buttonhole band.

Work in patt until band measures 1" (2.5 cm) from pick-up row. BO all sts in patt.

Weave in loose ends. Sew buttons to buttonband and neckband opposite buttonholes.

Tilghman Island
PULLOVER

DESIGNED BY COURTNEY KELLEY

Inspired by maritime life in the North Seas, this boatneck pullover features a diamond pattern across the yoke and a small allover pattern in the sleeves for a new twist on traditional Fair Isle patterns. The shape couldn't be more simple and traditional, but subtle waist shaping and a modified drop shoulder flatter the body. The sleeves have no shaping between the cuff and armhole, which makes them blousy at the cuff and fitted at the upper arm and gives a feminine touch that complements the strong blue-and-white color scheme. The lack of shaping at the yoke makes the allover Fair Isle pattern quick and easy to knit.

MATERIALS

yarn
Sportweight (#2 Fine).

shown here: The Fibre Company Savannah (50% wool, 20% cotton, 15% linen, 15% soy fiber; 160 yd [146 m]/50 g): bluegrass (MC), 8 (9, 10, 11, 12) skeins; natural (CC), 1 (1, 2, 2, 2) skein(s).

needles
body and sleeves: size U.S. 6 (4 mm): 24" (60 cm) circular (cir) and set of 4 or 5 double-pointed (dpn).

edging: size U.S. 5 (3.75 mm): 24" (60 cm) cir and set of 4 or 5 dpn.

Adjust needle size if necessary to obtain the correct gauge.

notions
Markers (m); stitch holders; tapestry needle.

gauge
23 stitches and 32 rounds = 4" (10 cm) in stockinette stitch on larger needle, worked in rounds.

finished size
About 29¼ (33½, 37½, 41¾, 46)" (74.5 [85, 95, 106, 117] cm) bust circumference. Pullover shown measures 33½" (85 cm).

Steeks

Steeks can be daunting, but, as with everything, there is a trade-off. A steek allows the knitter to work a sweater in rounds, then later cut the knitting to create a cardigan, armhole, or neck opening. A line or two of staystitches worked with a sewing machine (alternately you could use a crochet hook or needle and thread) guarantee that the knitting won't ravel when cut.

When preparing a steek for an armhole or neck, bind off the appropriate number of stitches as indicated in the pattern, then on the following round, cast on extra "steek" stitches so that you can continue to work in rounds. In general, you do not need to cast on as many stitches as were bound off—usually 5 to 7 steek stitches, or 1" (2.5 cm) of width, is sufficient. Knit these stitches in a simple stripe or checkerboard pattern with the yarns used in each round to help prevent the floats from getting too long and, more importantly, to provide a visual guide for your scissors later.

When you get to the shoulders, bind off the regular stitches as well as the steek stitches. To cut a steek, work as follows:

STEP 1. Baste a line of contrasting yarn or thread along the center of the center steek stitch (Figure 1).

STEP 2. Use a sewing machine set for a small straight stitch to sew one or two lines of stitches on each side of the marked center stitch (Figure 2) to ensure that the cut edges will not ravel.

STEP 3. Cut along the marked center stitch, being careful to stay between the sewing machine lines (Figure 3).

For this sweater, a facing is knitted in reverse stockinette stitch at the end of the sleeve, which, after the sleeve is sewn into the armhole, is sewn to the inside of the garment to cover the raw edges of the cut steek. Not only does this make the knitting look tidier on the inside, it protects the cut edges from any fraying due to wear and use.

figure 1

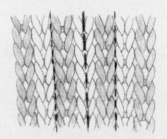

figure 2

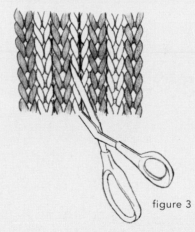

figure 3

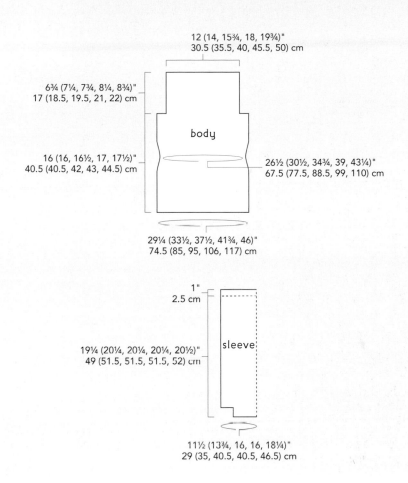

12 (14, 15¾, 18, 19¾)"
30.5 (35.5, 40, 45.5, 50) cm

6¾ (7¼, 7¾, 8¼, 8¾)"
17 (18.5, 19.5, 21, 22) cm

body

16 (16, 16½, 17, 17½)"
40.5 (40.5, 42, 43, 44.5) cm

26½ (30½, 34¾, 39, 43¼)"
67.5 (77.5, 88.5, 99, 110) cm

29¼ (33½, 37½, 41¾, 46)"
74.5 (85, 95, 106, 117) cm

1"
2.5 cm

19¼ (20¼, 20¼, 20¼, 20½)"
49 (51.5, 51.5, 51.5, 52) cm

sleeve

11½ (13¾, 16, 16, 18¼)"
29 (35, 40.5, 40.5, 46.5) cm

Body

With CC and smaller needle, CO 168 (192, 216, 240, 264) sts. Place marker (pm) and join for working in rnds, being careful not to twist sts. Rnd begs at side "seam." Change to MC and knit 1 rnd. Work in k2, p2 rib until piece measures 2" (5 cm) from CO, placing a second m after 84 (96, 108, 120, 132) sts to denote other side "seam." Change to larger needle and work even in St st (knit every rnd) for 1" (2.5 cm). Work Rnds 1–19 of Bottom Band chart. Work even in St st for 1" (2.5 cm) more.

DEC RND: K1, k2tog, knit to 3 sts before next m, ssk, k1, slip marker (sl m), k1, k2tog, knit to 3 sts before next m, ssk, k1—4 sts dec'd.

Work 5 (5, 5, 7, 7) rnds even. Rep the last 6 (6, 6, 8, 8) rnds 3 more times—152 (176, 200, 224, 248) sts rem.

Work even in St st until piece measures 1½ (1½, 2, 2½, 2½)" (3.8 [3.8, 5, 6.5, 6.5] cm) from last dec.

INC RND: K1, M1 (see page 78), knit to 1 st before next m, M1, k1, sl m, k1, M1, knit to 1 st before next m, M1, k1—4 sts inc'd.

Work 5 (5, 5, 7, 7) rnds even. Rep the last 6 (6, 6, 8, 8) rnds 3 more times—168 (192, 216, 240, 264) sts.

Work even until piece measures 16 (16, 16½, 17, 17½)" (40.5 [40.5, 42, 43, 44.5] cm) from CO or desired length to underarm, ending 7 (7, 8, 8, 9) sts before end-of-rnd m on last rnd.

Bottom Band

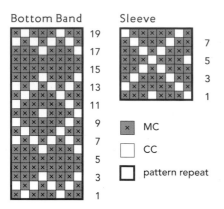

19
17
15
13
11
9
7
5
3
1

Sleeve

7
5
3
1

■ MC

□ CC

□ pattern repeat

Yoke

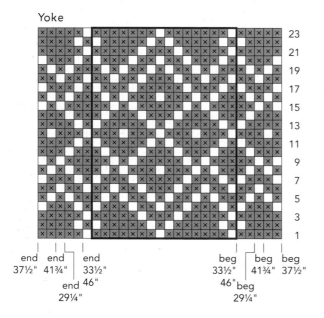

23
21
19
17
15
13
11
9
7
5
3
1

end 37½" end 41¾" end 33½"

end 46" end 29¼"

beg 33½" beg 41¾" beg 37½"

46" beg beg 29¼"

Divide for Front and Back

Removing markers as you come to them, BO 14 (14, 16, 16, 18) sts, knit to 7 (7, 8, 8, 9) sts before next m, BO 14 (14, 16, 16, 18) sts, knit to end of rnd—70 (82, 92, 104, 114) sts rem each for front and back.

SET-UP STEEK: Pm, use the backward-loop method (see Glossary) to CO 6 sts for steek (see sidebar on page 136), pm, knit to BO sts, pm, use the backward-loop method to CO 6 sts for steek, pm, knit to end of rnd.

Working each set of 6 steek sts as (k1, k1 through back loop (tbl), k2, k1tbl, k1) on every rnd, cont in St st until piece measures 2½ (3, 3½, 4, 4½)" (6.5 [7.5, 9, 10, 11.5] cm) from steek set-up.

NEXT RND: *Work to end of steek sts, sl m, k2tog; rep from * once more, kit to end of rnd—69 (81, 91, 103, 113) sts rem each for front and back; 6 sts for each steek.

Working each set of steek sts as (k1 MC, k1tbl CC, k2 MC, k1tbl CC, k1 MC) on every rnd and beg and ending as indicated for your size between each set of steek sts, work Rnds 1–23 of Yoke chart. Work even in MC for ¼" (6 mm).

Divide for Neckband

BO 6 steek sts, knit to next set of steek sts, BO 6 steek sts, knit to end of rnd—69 (81, 91, 103, 113) sts rem each for front and back. Working back and forth in rows on back sts only, cont as foll:

SET-UP ROW: (WS) P1, *k2, p2; rep from * to last 0 (0, 2, 2, 0) sts, k0 (0, 2, 2, 0).

Cont in rib as established until neckband measures 1" (2.5 cm), ending with a RS row. With CC, BO all sts in patt. Working back and froth in rows on front sts only, work rib as for back, ending with a WS row. With CC, BO all sts in patt.

Sleeves

With CC and smaller needles, CO 40 (48, 56, 56, 64) sts. Arrange sts as evenly as possible on 3 or 4 needles, pm, and join for working in rnds, being careful not to twist sts. Change to MC and work in k2, p2 rib until piece measures 1½" (3.8 cm) from CO. Change to larger needles and work k1f&b (see Glossary) in every st—80 (96, 112, 112, 128) sts. Rep Rnds 1–8 of Sleeve chart until piece measures 18 (19,

19, 19, 19)" (45.5 [48.5, 48.5, 48.5, 48.5] cm) from CO. Divide work at m and work back and forth in rows for 1¼ (1¼, 1¼, 1¼, 1½)" (3.2 [3.2, 3.2, 3.2, 3.8] cm) more. With MC, work in rev St st (purl RS rows; knit WS rows) for 1" (2.5 cm) for steek facing. BO all sts.

Finishing

Cut Steek

Using a sewing machine on the smallest straight-stitch setting, sew 2 lines of sts on the inside of the k1tbl CC sts for each steek. With sharp scissors, carefully cut between the sewing lines. Trim away extra fabric, leaving sewn sts intact.

Neckband

Fold the neckbands over one another at the shoulders so that the back band is on top of the front band and whipstitch (see Glossary) them tog at the outermost edges.

Seams

With MC threaded on a tapestry needle, use the mattress st (see Glossary) to sew sleeves into armholes, sewing split section at top of sleeve to BO edge of body underarm. Use whipstitches to sew steek facing to inside of body, covering cut steek edges.

Weave in loose ends. Block to measurements.

Vorderrhein HAT

DESIGNED BY KATE GAGNON OSBORN

Twisted-stitch cables—traveling cables comprised of intertwined one-stitch strands in which each stitch is knitted through the back loop—create a tight fabric with beautiful dimension and impressive texture. There is very little information regarding the first occurrence of this special type of cable patterning, but many consider the origin and inspiration to lay in the gnarly trees and deep forests of Germany. The rich pattern in this warm hat begins with a twisted rib that transforms into two alternating cable panels for the longer, slightly slouchy body. The crown is shaped with decreases that are integrated within the cables. A large pom-pom provides a full finish to the top.

MATERIALS

yarn
Worsted weight (#4 Medium).

shown here: The Fibre Company Organik (70% organic merino, 15% alpaca, 15% silk; 98 yd [90 m]/50 g): atoll (turquoise), 2 skeins.

needles
body: size U.S. 7 (4.5 mm): 16" (40 cm) circular (cir) and set of 4 or 5 double-pointed (dpn).

ribbing: size U.S. 5 (3.75 mm): 16" (40 cm) cir.

Adjust needle size if necessary to obtain the correct gauge.

notions
Markers (m); 2 cable needles (cn); pom-pom maker or cardboard for template; tapestry needle.

gauge
One cable pattern repeat (24 stitches) = 3¾" (9.5 cm) on larger needles, worked in rounds.

23 rounds = 4" (10 cm) in cable pattern, worked in rounds.

finished size
About 18¾" (47.5 cm) in circumference and 9¼" (23.5 cm) long, excluding pom-pom. To fit an adult.

Cabling without a Cable Needle

This project is perfect for learning how to work cables without a cable needle, as the vast majority of the cables use only two stitches, which reduces the potential for dropped stitches. For ease of explanation, the directions below describe how to work a 1/1 cable, but the same principles can be applied to cables involving more stitches.

STEP 1. Slip the first stitch off of the left-hand needle and let it drop (Figure 1) in the front of the work for a left-leaning cable or in the back of the work for a right-leaning cable.

STEP 2. Slip the next stitch onto the right-hand needle to temporarily hold it, keeping the dropped stitch in front (Figure 2) or back.

STEP 3. Return the dropped stitch to the left-hand needle, then return the held stitch from the right-hand needle to the left-hand needle (Figure 3).

STEP 4. Work these 2 stitches in their new order (Figure 4) to complete the cable.

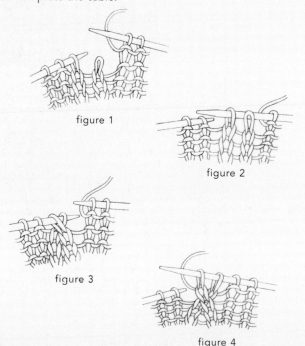

figure 1

figure 2

figure 3

figure 4

Hat

With smaller cir needle, CO 100 sts. Place marker (pm) and join for working in rnds, being careful not to twist sts. Work Rnd 1 of Ribbing chart 11 times—piece measures about 1½" (3.8 cm) from CO. Work Rnds 2 and 3 of Ribbing chart—120 sts.

Change to larger cir needle.

Work Rnds 1–16 of Cable chart 2 times.

Work Rnds 1–10 of Cable Decrease chart, changing to dpn when there are too few sts to fit comfortably on cir needle—30 sts rem.

NEXT RND: *K1 through back loop (tbl), p1, sl 1 pwise, k2tog, psso, p1; rep from *—20 sts rem.

NEXT RND: *Sl 1 pwise, k1, psso; rep from *—10 sts rem.

Finishing

Cut yarn, leaving an 8" (20.5 cm) tail. Thread tail through rem sts, pull tight to close hole, and fasten off on WS. Block lightly.

Pom-Pom

Make a 2" (5 cm) pom-pom with remaining yarn, using a pom-pom maker or as foll: Cut a piece of cardboard 2" (5 cm) square. Cut a 12" (30.5 cm) length of yarn for tying pom-pom later. Wrap rem yarn around cardboard—more wraps will make a fuller pom-pom. Slide wraps off of cardboard and use 12" (30.5 cm) length to tie tightly at center. Cut loops and fluff pom-pom. Using tails from tying pom-pom, sew pom-pom securely to top of hat. Weave in loose ends.

Cable

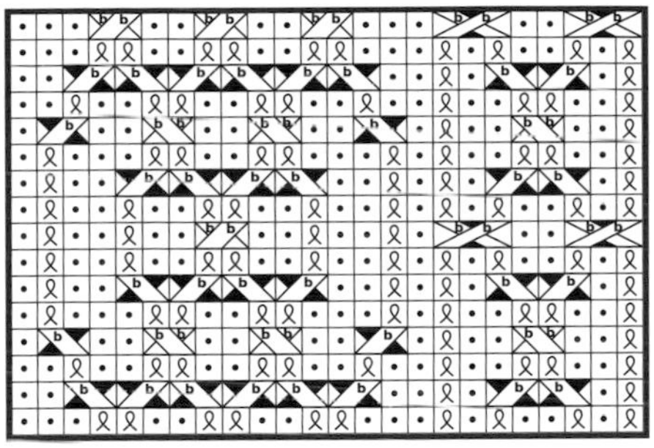

15
13
11
9
7
5
3
1

Cable Decrease

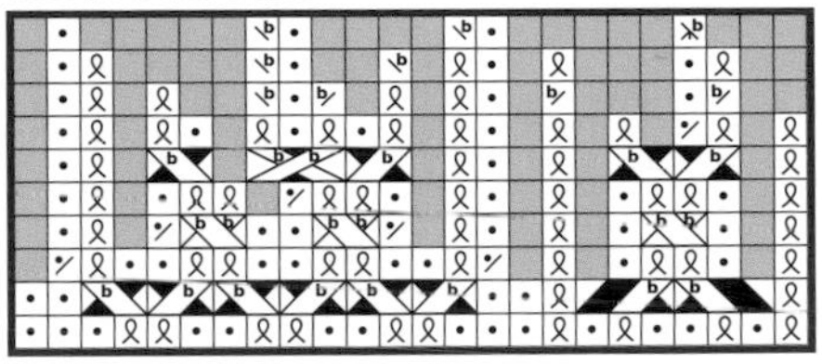

9
7
5
3
1

Ribbing

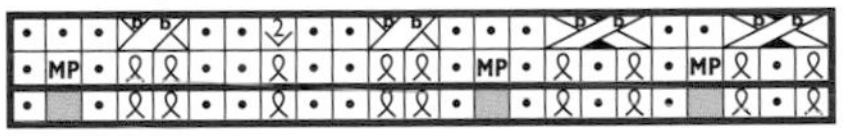

3
1

ℛ	k1tbl
·	purl
↘	p2tog
ᵇ	sl 2 sts pwise, [sl 1 st to left needle by inserting left needle tip from right to left into st] 2 times, k2tog
↖	k2tog tbl
⋏	sl 1 pwise, k2tog, psso
MP	M1 pwise (see Glossary)
↲	k1f&b (see Glossary)
▨	no stitch
☐	pattern repeat

sl 1 st onto cn, hold in back, k1tbl, k1tbl from cn

sl 1 st onto cn, hold in front, k1tbl, k1tbl from cn

sl 1 st onto cn, hold in back, k1tbl, p1 from cn

sl 1 st onto cn, hold in front, p1, k1tbl from cn

sl 1 st onto cn, hold in back, k1tbl, sl st from cn to left needle, p2tog

sl 1 st onto cn, hold in back, sl 1 st onto 2nd cn, hold in front, sl st from first cn to left needle, p2tog, k1tbl from cn

sl 1 st onto cn, hold in back, sl 1 st onto 2nd cn, hold in back, k1tbl, p1 from 2nd cn, k1tbl from first cn

Ajiro SCARF

DESIGNED BY COURTNEY KELLEY

This scarf was inspired by a picture in *Handschuhe,* a vintage knitting book from Germany by Eva Maria Leszner. The basketweave pattern is reminiscent of fishing nets, so I chose blue and natural colors to accentuate the ideas of sea and shore. The Japanese word *ajiro* describes a herringbone pattern in basketry, which seems fitting for a country known for its long fishing traditions and bold graphic representations of natural elements. This scarf is knitted in the round, which simplifies the Fair Isle patterning (no wrong-side rows) and creates an insulating double layer of fabric. This scarf will keep you warm even on the coldest windswept shore.

MATERIALS

yarn
Sportweight (#2 Fine).

shown here: The Fibre Company Road to China Light (65% baby alpaca, 15% silk, 10% cashmere, 10% camel, 159 yd [145 m]/50 g): riverstone (MC), 3 skeins; aquamarine (CC), 2 skeins

needles
body: size U.S. 4 (3.5 mm): 16" (40 cm) circular (cir).

edging: size U.S. 3 (3.25 mm): 16" (40 cm) cir.

Adjust needle size if necessary to obtain the correct gauge.

notions
Contrasting waste yarn and size E/4 (3.5 mm) crochet hook for provisional CO; markers (m); tapestry needle.

gauge
32 stitches and 25 rounds = 4" (10 cm) in charted pattern on larger needles, worked in rounds.

finished size
About 6" (15 cm) wide and 55" (139.5 cm) long, after blocking.

Tacking Long Floats

When working a stranded pattern, you never want to carry the non-working yarn across the back of the work for more than about 5 stitches, or whatever constitutes about a inch at your gauge. Some patterns, such as the Ajiro Scarf, require that the non-working yarn is carried farther—7 stitches in this case. To help shorten the floats while maintaining good tension, "tack" these long floats to the wrong side of the work.

STEP 1. Knit 2 or 3 stitches with MC (2 stitches shown in illustration), insert the right-hand needle tip into the next stitch on the left-hand needle, place the non-working yarn (in this case, CC) over the right-hand needle (Figure 1), then knit the stitch with the working yarn (in this case, MC) as usual.

STEP 2. Lower the non-working yarn and knit the next stitch to trap the non-working yarn against the back of the fabric (Figure 2).

As with any stranded pattern, keep the floats nice and loose against the wrong side of the knitted fabric.

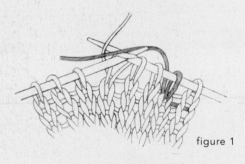

figure 1

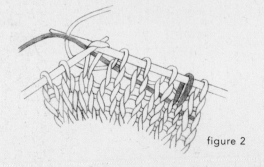

figure 2

Scarf

With contrasting waste yarn, CC, and larger 16" (40 cm) cir needle, use the crochet method (see Glossary) to provisionally CO 98 sts. Place marker (pm) and join for working in rnds, being careful not to twist sts.

NEXT RND: Work 49 sts according to Rnd 1 of Ajiro chart, pm, beg at right edge of chart, work 49 sts according to Rnd 1 of chart again.

Cont as established, rep Rnds 1–12 of Ajiro chart until piece measures about 54" (137 cm) from CO, ending with Rnd 1 or Rnd 7 of chart. Change to smaller cir needle and CC. Knit 1 rnd.

Finishing

Place 49 front sts onto one needle and 49 back sts onto a second needle. Holding the needles parallel in your left hand and holding the other end of the smaller cir needle in your right hand, use CC to knit the sts tog as foll: *Insert right needle tip into the first st on the front needle, then into the first st on the back needle, then knit these sts tog, rep from * to end—49 sts rem.

Work 4 rows in garter st (knit every row). BO all sts.

Carefully remove waste yarn from provisional CO and repeat finishing instructions for other end.

Ajiro

				×	×	×		×			V
					×				×		
			×						×		V
×				×					×		
×	×		×					×	×	×	V
×	×	×					×	×	×	×	
×	×					×		×	×	×	V
×					×						
	×						×				V
		×			×	×					
			×	×	×	×	×				V

11
9
7
5
3
1

- ☐ MC
- ☒ CC
- ☑ sl 1 pwise wyb
- ☐ pattern repeat

GLOSSARY

Abbreviations

beg   begin(s); beginning
BO   bind off
CC   contrasting color
cir   circular
cm   centimeter(s)
cn   cable needle
CO   cast on
cont   continue(s); continuing
dec(s)   decrease(s); decreasing
dpn   double-pointed needles
foll   follow(s); following
g   gram(s)
inc(s)   increase(s); increasing
k   knit
kwise   knitwise, as if to knit
k1f&b   knit into the front and back of same stitch
m   marker(s)
MC   main color
mm   millimeter(s)

M1   make one (increase)
p   purl
patt(s)   pattern(s)
psso   pass slipped stitch over
pwise   purlwise, as if to purl
p1f&b   purl into front and back of same stitch
rem   remain(s); remaining
rep   repeat(s); repeating
rev St st reverse stockinette stitch
rnd(s)   round(s)
RS   right side
sl   slip
sl st   slip st (slip 1 stitch purlwise unless otherwise indicated)
ssk   slip 2 stitches knitwise, one at a time, from left needle to right needle, insert left needle tip through both front loops and knit together from this position (1 stitch decrease)

st(s)   stitch(es)
St st   stockinette stitch
tbl   through back loop
tog   together
WS   wrong side
wyb   with yarn in back
wyf   with yarn in front
yd   yard(s)
yo   yarnover
*   repeat starting point
* *   repeat all instructions between asterisks
( )   alternate measurements and/ or instructions
[ ]   work instructions as a group a specified number of times

BIND-OFFS

Three-Needle Bind-Off

Place the stitches to be joined onto two separate needles and hold the needles parallel so that the right sides of knitting face together. Insert a third needle into the first stitch on each of two needles (Figure 1) and knit them together as one stitch (Figure 2), *knit the next stitch on each needle the same way, then use the left needle tip to lift the first stitch over the second and off the needle (Figure 3). Repeat from * until no stitches remain on first two needles. Cut yarn and pull tail through last stitch to secure.

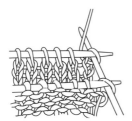
figure 1

figure 2

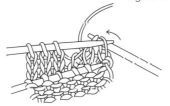
figure 3

Two-Stitch One-Row Buttonhole

Note: Illustrations show a four-stitch buttonhole; instructions are for a two-stitch buttonhole.

Bring the yarn to the front of the work, slip the next stitch purlwise, then return the yarn to the back. *Slip the next stitch, pass the second stitch over the slipped stitch and drop it off the needle (Figure 1). Repeat from * once more. Slip the last stitch on the right needle to the left needle and turn the work around. Bring the working yarn to the back, [insert the right needle between the first and second stitches on the left needle (Figure 2), draw up a loop and place it on the left needle] 3 times. Turn the work around. With the yarn in back, slip the first stitch and pass the extra cast-on stitch over it (Figure 3) and off the needle to complete the buttonhole.

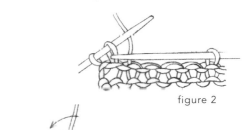
figure 1

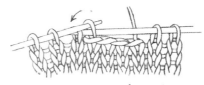
figure 2

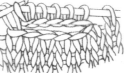
figure 3

Backward-Loop Cast-On

*Loop working yarn and place it on needle backward so that it doesn't unwind. Repeat from *.

Cable Cast-On

If there are no stitches on the needles, make a slipknot of working yarn and place it on the needle, then use the knitted method to cast-on one more stitch—two stitches on needle. Hold needle with working yarn in your left hand. *Insert right needle between the first two stitches on left needle (Figure 1), wrap yarn around needle as if to knit, draw yarn through (Figure 2), and place new loop on left needle (Figure 3) to form a new stitch. Repeat from * for the desired number of stitches, always working between the last stitch made and the stitch next to it.

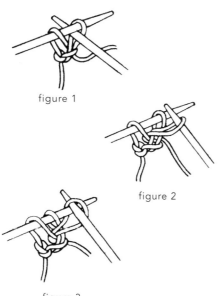

figure 1

figure 2

figure 3

Crochet Chain Provisional Cast-On

With waste yarn and crochet hook, make a loose crochet chain (see page 153) about four stitches more than you need to cast on. With knitting needle, working yarn, and beginning two stitches from end of chain, pick up and knit one stitch through the bump on the back of each crochet chain (Figure 1) for desired number of stitches. When you're ready to work in the opposite direction, pull out the crochet chain to expose live stitches (Figure 2).

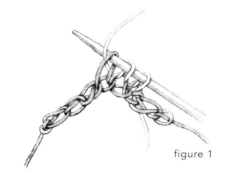

figure 1

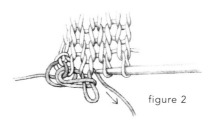

figure 2

Invisible Provisional Cast-On

Make a loose slipknot of working yarn and place it on the right needle. Hold a length of contrasting waste yarn next to the slipknot and around your left thumb; hold working yarn over your left index finger. *Bring the right needle forward, then under waste yarn, over working yarn, grab a loop of working yarn and bring it forward under waste yarn (Figure 1), then bring needle back behind the working yarn and grab a second loop (Figure 2). Repeat from * for the desired number of stitches. When you're ready to work in the opposite direction, place the exposed loops on a knitting needle as you pull out the waste yarn.

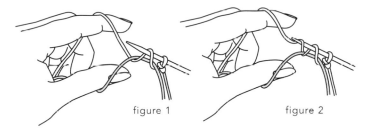

figure 1   figure 2

Crochet Chain (ch)

Make a slipknot and place it on crochet hook if there isn't a loop already on the hook. *Yarn over hook and draw through loop on hook. Repeat from * for the desired number of stitches. To fasten off, cut yarn and draw end through last loop formed.

Knitted Cast-On

Make a slipknot and place it on the left needle if there are no stitches already there. *Use the right needle to knit the first stitch (or slipknot) on left needle (Figure 1) and place new loop onto left needle to form a new stitch (Figure 2). Repeat from * for the desired number of stitches, always working into the last stitch made.

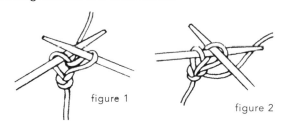

figure 1   figure 2

DECREASES

Slip, Slip, Knit (ssk)

Slip two stitches individually knitwise (Figure 1), insert left needle tip into the front of these two slipped stitches, and use the right needle to knit them together through their back loops (Figure 2).

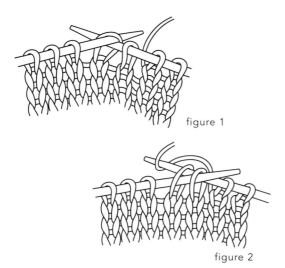

figure 1

figure 2

Slip, Slip, Purl (ssp)

Holding yarn in front, slip two stitches individually knitwise (Figure 1), then slip these two stitches back onto left needle (they will be turned on the needle) and purl them together through their back loops (Figure 2).

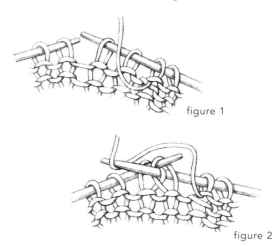

figure 1

figure 2

Slip, Slip, Slip, Knit (sssk)

Slip three stitches individually knitwise, insert left needle tip into the front of all three slipped stitches, and use the right needle to knit them together through their back loops.

Kitchener Stitch

Arrange stitches on two needles so that there is the same number of stitches on each needle. Hold the needles parallel to each other with right sides of the knitting facing up. Allowing about ½" (1.3 cm) per stitch to be grafted, thread matching yarn on a tapestry needle. Work from right to left as follows:

STEP 1. Bring tapestry needle through the first stitch on the front needle as if to purl and leave the stitch on the needle (Figure 1).

STEP 2. Bring tapestry needle through the first stitch on the back needle as if to knit and leave that stitch on the needle (Figure 2).

STEP 3. Bring tapestry needle through the first front stitch as if to knit and slip this stitch off the needle, then bring tapestry needle through the next front stitch as if to purl and leave this stitch on the needle (Figure 3).

STEP 4. Bring tapestry needle through the first back stitch as if to purl and slip this stitch off the needle, then bring tapestry needle through the next back stitch as if to knit and leave this stitch on the needle (Figure 4).

Repeat Steps 3 and 4 until one stitch remains on each needle, adjusting the tension to match the rest of the knitting as you go. To finish, bring tapestry needle through the front stitch as if to knit and slip this stitch off the needle, then bring tapestry needle through the back stitch as if to purl and slip this stitch off the needle.

Grafting for Garter Stitch
See page 84.

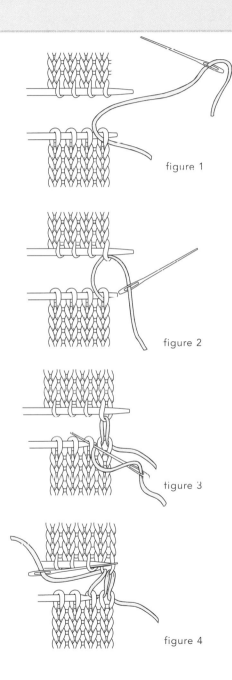

figure 1

figure 2

figure 3

figure 4

INCREASES

Bar Increase Knitwise (k1f&b)

Knit into a stitch but leave it on the left needle (Figure 1), then knit through the back loop of the same stitch (Figure 2) and slip the original stitch off the needle (Figure 3).

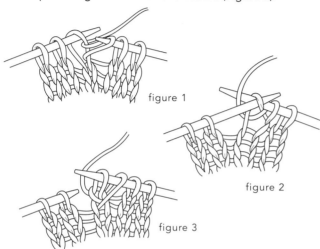

figure 1

figure 2

figure 3

Bar Increase Purlwise (p1f&b)

Purl into a stitch but leave the stitch on the left needle (Figure 1), then purl through the back loop of the same stitch (Figure 2) and slip the original stitch off the needle.

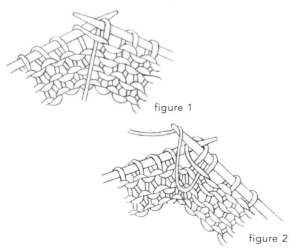

figure 1

figure 2

Raised Make-One Increase (M1)

See page 78.

Raised Increase Purlwise (M1P)

With left needle tip, lift the strand between the needles from front to back (Figure 1), then purl the lifted loop through the back (Figure 2).

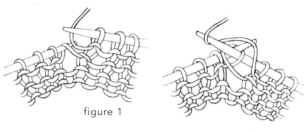

figure 1

figure 2

Pick Up and Purl

With wrong side of work facing and working from right to left, *insert needle tip under selvedge stitch from the far side to the near side (Figure 1), wrap yarn around needle, and pull a loop through (Figure 2). Repeat from * for desired number of stitches.

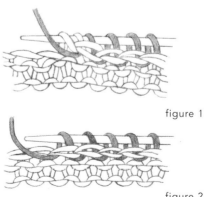

figure 1

figure 2

SEAMS

Mattress Stitch

Place the pieces to be seamed on a table, right sides facing up. Begin at the lower edge and work upward as follows for your stitch pattern:

Stockinette Stitch with 1-Stitch Seam Allowance

Insert threaded needle under one bar between the two edge stitches on one piece, then under the corresponding bar plus the bar above it on the other piece (Figure 1). *Pick up the next two bars on the first piece (Figure 2), then the next two bars on the other (Figure 3). Repeat from *, ending by picking up the last bar or pair of bars on the first piece.

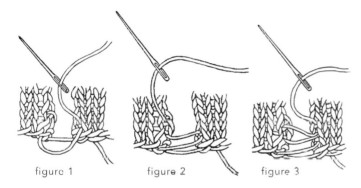

figure 1   figure 2   figure 3

Stockinette Stitch with ½-Stitch Seam Allowance

To reduce bulk in the mattress-stitch seam, work as for the 1-stitch seam allowance but pick up the bars in the center of the edge stitches instead of between the last two stitches.

Whipstitch

Hold pieces to be sewn together so that the edges to be seamed are even with each other. With yarn threaded on a tapestry needle, *insert needle through both layers from back to front, then bring needle to back. Repeat from *, keeping even tension on the seaming yarn.

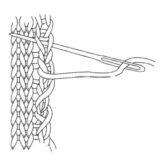

SOURCES FOR YARN

All of the yarns in this book are from The Fibre
Company and are distributed by Kelbourne Woolens.

Kelbourne Woolens

915 North 28th Street, second floor
Philadelphia, PA 19130
kelbournewoolens.com

INDEX

Check out these resources from Interweave
with even more chic and contemporary
knitted garments and accessories

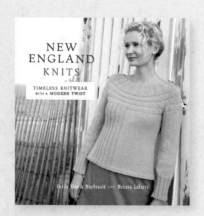

New England Knits
Timeless Knitwear with
a Modern Twist
*Cecily Glowik MacDonald
and Melissa LaBarre*
ISBN 978-1-59668-180-4
$24.95

French Girl Knits
Innovative Techniques, Romantic
Details, and Feminine Designs
Kristeen Griffin-Grimes
ISBN 978-1-59668-069-2
$24.95

Inspired to Knit
Creating Exquisite Handknits
Michele Rose Orne
ISBN 978-1-59668-041-8
$24.95

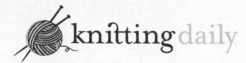

Join KnittingDaily.com, an online community that
shares your passion for knitting. You'll get a free e-
newsletter, free patterns, projects store, a daily blog,
even updates, galleries, tips and techniques, and
more. Sign up for *Knitting Daily* at knittingdaily.com.

KNITS
INTERWEAVE

From cover to cover, *Interweave Knits* magazine pres-
ents great projects for the beginner to the advanced
knitter. Every issue is packed full of captivating smart
designs, step-by-step instructions, easy-to-understand
illustrations, plus well-written, lively articles sure to
inspire. Interweaveknits.com

INTERWEAVE
interweave.com